*Back in
Charge!*

Back in Charge!

A Guide to Harnessing
the Magic of Your Brain
to Create the Life You'll Love

ADRIANNE AHERN, PH.D.

SENTIENT PUBLICATIONS

I dedicate this book to my grandniece Aurora Ahern Carlsen,
whose gift of light opens my heart.

First Sentient Publications edition 2009

Copyright © 2009 by Adrianne Ahern, PhD

A paperback original

Cover design by Blair O'Neil
Cover photo by Blair O'Neil
Book design by Timm Bryson

Library of Congress Cataloging-in-Publication Data

Ahern, Adrianne, 1960–
Back in charge : A guide to harnessing the magic of your brain to create
the life you'll love / Adrianne Ahern.
p. cm.
ISBN 978-1-59181-089-6 (alk. paper)
1. Mind and body. 2. Self-perception. 3. Self-actualization (Psychology)
I. Title.
BF161.A34 2009
158.1--dc22
2009000762

Printed in the United States of America

10 9 8 7 6 5 4 3 2 1

SENTIENT PUBLICATIONS
A Limited Liability Company
1113 Spruce Street
Boulder, CO 80302
www.sentientpublications.com

CONTENTS

8   Pulling It All Together: Rewiring in a Nutshell   115

Epilogue: Beyond Conditioning   135

About the Author

INTRODUCTION

In the 1960s, a rare and beautiful white tiger, Mohini, was given to President Eisenhower as a gift. This magnificent young tiger was sent to live in the National Zoo in Washington, D.C., where, as was typical of zoos at that time, she was put into a twelve-foot by twelve-foot cage with a hard concrete floor and heavy steel bars spaced apart just far enough so visitors could see in—but Mohini could not get out. For many years, Mohini spent her days pacing back and forth in an endless figure eight, brushing against the bars of her cage. In time, a wealthy benefactor took pity on this wonderful creature and gave the zoo enough money to build her a more natural habitat: several acres of trees, hills, and caves with a pond and grassy areas. The media was called in and stood poised to film Mohini's first moments in her lovely new surroundings. And do you know what Mohini did? As soon as she entered her beautiful, spacious habitat, she dashed to a far corner by the wall and marked off a twelve-foot square for herself. She stayed in that square, pacing until the area was worn bare, for the rest of her days.

This is a poignant example of *classic conditioning*. Mohini was a magnificent, beautiful, powerful creature who was convinced that she must live within the boundaries of her invisible twelve by twelve cage. Despite the abundant space all around her, she confined herself to much less. Staying within that small space wasn't just a fleeting idea to her, but surely she felt as if her very survival depended on it. I'm certain that whenever Mohini even thought of leaving her small area, her heartbeat raced, her breathing became labored, and her entire physiology told her it was unsafe.

> Every child is an artist. The problem is how to remain an artist once he grows up.
>
> —*Pablo Picasso*

Classic conditioning doesn't just occur in tigers or hamsters or Pavlov's dogs. We humans run our lives by it also. Conditioning itself is benign, neutral. It is the way in which the brain organizes its power to move us toward what we desire or to affirm what we believe to be true. Conditioning can support mental/emotional cages that limit life experience (as in Mohini's case) or unleash unlimited potential. *Conscious empowering conditioning* can often overcome cages that most of us would consider quite real and unconquerable, as exemplified by Helen Keller.

Helen Keller was deaf and blind from infancy, yet this brilliant woman graduated magna cum laude from Radcliffe in 1904 and could read in five languages. During her long active lifetime, she wrote twelve books and many articles, and became an international speaker and an influential political activist, helping to found the American Civil Liberties Union. She was awarded the Presidential Medal of Freedom and lived a rich and full life. Helen Keller, against all odds, freed her Mohini from the barriers that many would consider insurmountable.

How did she do it? With the help of a dedicated teacher, Helen Keller used *conscious conditioning,* beliefs deeply embedded in her brain, to determine the course of her life. To get a glimpse of what those critical beliefs were, here's what Helen Keller had to say about life:

Be of good cheer. Do not think of today's failures, but of the success that may come tomorrow.

You have set yourself a difficult task, but you will succeed if you persevere; and you will find a joy in overcoming obstacles.

We can do anything we want to if we stick to it long enough.

It is for us to pray not for tasks equal to our powers, but for powers equal to our tasks, to go forward with a great desire forever beating at the door of our hearts as we travel toward our distant goal.

In this book, I want to convince you of three things: First, that we are all Mohinis—magnificent, powerful, beautiful—whether we acknowledge it or not. Second, that the mental/emotional cages that hold us back are not *real* limitations but unconscious, nonproductive conditioning that has been hardwired into our brains. And third, that you can use the recent discoveries of neuropsychology, which come together in the form of the four steps of the Snap Out of it NOW! Method, to retrain your brain so that its incredible power can support whatever you desire to be, do, and have out of life.

Cages come in different sizes. A world-class athlete may feel caged because she can't seem to break her own record. A salesperson may feel caged because no matter how much energy he puts into his job, he just can't seem to close his quota of sales. You may feel caged because of feelings of complacency that seem to block you from doing the things you know you should be doing to achieve your dreams. We all have cages. But the good news is that once we understand our cages for what they are—merely the conditioning of our brains—we can dismantle them.

To Reap the Benefits...

To truly experience the transformation waiting for you, you will want to approach this book as an experiential workshop rather than a theoretical lecture. Read the chapters and examples with the sense that they are about *you*. Resist the temptation to apply this knowledge to how you perceive your neighbor or cousin or significant other.

Take the time to really experience the Snap Out of it NOW! exercises for yourself and ruminate over the questions. The exercises are intended to give you an experiential understanding of the concepts so you can apply them to your life effectively. Rather than inhaling the facts of the science, absorb the feeling of the practices. The exercises and practices are described within these pages, but also on the accompanying CDs with additional explanation and guidance. I'd recommend that you read the chapters in order, then at the end of each, pause and listen to the CD tracks related to that chapter and do the exercises. (For some chapters there are exercises on the CD that are in addition to the ones in this book.) Some may seem difficult. Some may seem simplistic. But don't skip over any! In fact, you'll want to do many of them more than once to reap the benefits.

This isn't magic; it's neuroscience. And the goal of this book and its accompanying CDs is to make this science accessible to you on a practical level so you can create magical results and free your own Mohini.

Chapter 1

Bridging the Chasm

*Warning: The contents of this book may,
unlike previous self-improvement prescriptions you have taken,
actually change your life and help you attain your goals.*

Looking Across the Chasm

We can see it: that bright future, those wonderful possibilities life has to offer. We can almost taste what it would feel like to attain our desires. And yet for many of us, our goals and dreams remain elusive. We get inspired by the latest motivational speaker or sure-fire improvement plan. But more often than not, we slip back into the same old ruts.

Have you tried a myriad of self-improvement programs? Struggled to correct bad habits or tap your potential? Have you spent hours affirming abundance, joy, and health only to manifest lack, boredom, and illness?

Let me tell you a secret that every life coach, human potential guru, and motivational speaker knows: *self-improvement programs rarely work in the long run.* Whether it's about losing weight or getting comfortable making sales calls, we just don't seem to make much headway no matter how many

A study commissioned by Medicare, published in the *American Psychologist* (Traci Mann, A. Janet Tomiyama, Erika Westling, Ann-Marie Lew, Barbra Samuels, Jason Chatman, "Medicare's Search for Effective Obesity Treatments: Diets Are Not the Answer," Vol. 62, No. 3, April 2007: 220-233) found that one-third to two-thirds of obese dieters regained more than they lost within a one-year period. The authors, a group of UCLA researchers, found that only a small minority of dieters sustained weight loss while the vast majority regained all of their weight and more.

Human potential gurus don't often discuss this, but it's true, despite the fact that you have desires and goals you are eager to achieve, despite the fact that you know that your life is not working out as it could or you are living a life that is very painful to you, and despite the hundreds or thousands of dollars and countless hours you've spent trying to make positive changes. Despite your intelligence, sincerity, and determination, you will still run into resistance when you begin the practices that I know (and research has proven) can make a tremendous difference in your life. Why?

techniques we try. I call it the chasm: that huge divide between your current reality and who you wish to be. Whether it's losing weight, attracting a lover, creating the career we desire, or improving our golf game, more often than not we don't bridge this huge gap and fall short of getting where we want to be.

It isn't that we're lazy or stupid or unmotivated. It isn't because what we desire to have or be or do is impossible. It isn't even because the self-improvement programs out there are invalid. It's because the internal mechanism—*our brain's conditioning*—that needs to be modified to create lasting change is the very same internal me chanism that is resisting the change we are trying to make!

It's a Catch-22, right? The very thing that needs to change so you can reach your goals is the same thing that will fight that change. All of the improvements you wish to make or goals you desire to reach are perfectly attainable for you except for one thing: Your brain will reject them.

Similar to the way that your body will reject a donor organ that is incompatible, your brain will activate all of its power to battle against any thoughts, ideas, or possibilities that feel foreign or incompatible to it. If you're convinced that you are disorganized, your brain will enlist its awesome

> If you can find a path with no obstacles, it probably doesn't lead anywhere.
>
> —*Frank A. Clark*

force to ensure that no time or space efficiency program in the world will work for you. If you believe that you are unattractive, your brain will make sure you see "ugly" in the mirror no matter how many plastic surgeries you have. Are you convinced that weight loss is difficult? Your brain will make sure that it is *impossible* for you!

Your brain is just doing its job. Your brain's job is to make sure that all of your systems—your visual perception, hormones, blood flow, breathing, muscle movements, emotions, et cetera—respond to and support *what you believe to be true*. It works overtime, diligently producing the reality you accept as valid.

So how does the brain know what you believe to be true? Your brain refers to the beliefs that have been *conditioned* or hardwired into it. We'll delve into the mechanics and dynamics of conditioning in the next chapter.

A study was commissioned by Werner Erhard and Associates (Jeffrey D. Fisher, Roxane Cohen Silver, Jack M. Chinsky, Barry Goff, Yechiel Klar, and Cyndi Zagieboylo, "Psychological effects of participation in a large group awareness training," *Journal of Consulting and Clinical Psychology*, Vol 57[6], Dec 1989: 747-755) regarding the effectiveness of large group awareness training, specifically those who had attended The Forum, the successor to the est training (Erhard Seminars Training, an personal transformation program founded by Werner H. Erhard) and at present the most widespread program for advancing human potential. The study concluded that The Forum had minimal lasting effects, positive or negative, on participants' self-perception.

But for now, think of conditioning as a set of deep-seated, oft-repeated, unwavering, and undeniable beliefs. These aren't just random or fleeting thoughts; conditioned beliefs are embedded in your physiology. They affect everything from your heartbeat to your hearing, your sweat glands to your sense of smell.

Whether unconscious or conscious, your conditioned beliefs determine your life path. They hold the key to your joy and misery. Your *conditioning* is the insidious force that controls your life—usually without your knowledge or permission. And, via the awesome power of your brain, your conditioning will block anything that runs counter to it. It can be your very best friend or your most powerful foe.

Scary, huh?

Truth is, it's only scary if we don't understand conditioning and don't know how to work with it. In the next chapters, I'll:

1. Help you understand what conditioning is and how it works

2. Show you how to discover *your own specific* conditioning and how it is running (or ruining) your life

3. Train you to consciously change your conditioning.

The point is to get your conditioning to work *for* you, not *against* you, to align your conditioning and the awesome power of your brain with what you desire.

So how do you know if your conditioned beliefs are supporting your efforts toward your goals or sabotaging them? In general, if you're having trouble making a change that is important to you, there is some conditioned belief blocking you. And that limiting conditioned belief could take a number of forms.

Disbelief in Change

Though many of us yearn for positive change and transformation, our conscious or unconscious conditioned beliefs may tell us that we really do not have the ability to become substantially different or better than who we have been. Do any of these statements ring true to you?

You can't teach an old dog new tricks.
This is just the way life is; we have to accept it.
You have to be born in the right place at the right time to make it.
You have to get the breaks and the right circumstances to be successful.
You can't have it all. Getting by is good enough.
Most of us just aren't cut out for greatness.

Some of us firmly believe these statements to be true. Others claim that they believe in unlimited human potential. But when it gets right down to it, almost all of us honestly *experience* life in terms of one or more of the limiting statements above.

Human potential is the *hope,* but life's limitations feel like the *reality.*

You may not ever say these statements out loud. You may even argue against them, using the positive self-talk of recent decades. But take a moment: In your heart of hearts, do any of those statements seem like the

---

EXERCISE: **What Popped Your Balloon?**

Note: All of the exercises in this book are also on the accompanying CD.

Take a moment to think about something you've tried to change or improve in the past. It could be putting more money into savings, exercising more regularly, or overcoming shyness. We usually start out an improvement program with a bang then fade in our enthusiasm. Remember back to when your enthusiasm was fading. Do any of these sound familiar? "Circumstances are in the way. I won't be able to _____ until my circumstances change." "Being _____ is just in my DNA. I can't change that." "If _____ was meant to be, it wouldn't feel so hard." Maybe you can't remember a conscious message, but can you remember how you felt? Discouraged? Resigned? This is your conditioned beliefs at work to keep you stuck!

whole truth and nothing but the truth? Deep down, do you trust these "reality" statements more than the possibility of transformation? If so, these beliefs have been hardwired into your brain and will sabotage any personal growth program you begin—and probably have done so in the past.

I am not asking you to just believe and trust in the possibility of your own transformation. Those limiting "reality" statements, like all conditioning, are hardwired in and need to be unplugged and rewired to release their power. I'll show you how to do this in future chapters, but for now I ask only that you hold them lightly and stay open.

The Known Is Painful—But the Unknown Is Terrifying!

Maybe you really *do* believe that you can transform yourself. But as sincerely as you *want* to change, the hardwiring of your brain is certain that you really *should not* change!

One of the most basic functions of the brain is survival: making sure that we stay out of harm's way. And if we do find ourselves in danger, our brains will work as hard as they can to get us back to safety. This survival instinct supersedes just about any other function of the brain.

Change of any kind means uncertainty, perhaps losing control of a life that you are just barely able to manage. Your current life may not be perfect, but it's familiar. Your brain has invested much time and energy learning to cope and adapt to this life of yours. Many of us feel that we are stretched so thin by our adapting and coping that any additional change would send us over the edge!

> Only those who risk going too far can possibly find out how far they can go.
>
> —*T. S. Eliot*

Philosophers often say that we are fearful of the unknown. In my opinion, we are much more frightened by the *loss of the known*. We think and say that we want to make more money, have happier and more romantic relationships, be less stressed at work, have more time with our children, have a healthy and attractive physique. But more strongly than all of this, we want to survive—and most of us are pretty darn good at knowing how to survive under our current circumstances. It's tough to give that up.

> One can choose to go back toward safety or forward toward growth. Growth must be chosen again and again; fear must be overcome again and again.
>
> —*Abraham Maslow*

For instance, on the surface, attaining extraordinary professional success certainly doesn't appear to threaten your survival. But what if unconsciously you connect being at the top with loneliness? What if you believe that this success will require a crazy time commitment and create painful imbalance in your life? What if you hold an underlying belief that highly successful people in your profession have to be slightly unethical or at least cutthroat? These deep-seated, often unconscious beliefs notify your brain that becoming a professional success is indeed very dangerous to your well-being.

In truth, change is inevitable. As Helen Keller said, "Life is either a daring adventure or nothing at all. Security is mostly a superstition. It does not exist in nature." No one, no circumstance, no state remains totally static—so you might as well choose your changes! But conscious change usually means stepping out of your comfort zone, that invisible twelve-foot cage that your brain perceives as safe for you. In the next chapters, I will give you techniques to help you to feel the fear and make the change you want anyway.

Specific Negative Beliefs

You undoubtedly have conditioned limiting beliefs specific to that aspect of yourself you would like to change. Keep in mind that a conditioned belief isn't just a light or fleeting thought. It feels and seems to be the truth. Do any of these sound familiar?

- I just wasn't born with the talent, intelligence, or raw ability to be, do, or have what I want.
- Genetically, I'm predisposed to be overweight/unhealthy/a loner/bad with numbers/nervous in front of people.
- To get my desires, I'd have to be credentialed/have more money/be physically stronger/be better looking/be smarter.
- Maybe if I'd started earlier in life, but now it's too late to go after my dreams.

In my years of practice, I've heard all kinds of limiting beliefs, from "But I've always been the fat one in my family" to "I just don't have enough killer instinct to be successful." Whether conscious or unconscious, these specific deep-seated beliefs will definitely take up arms to fight any effort to contradict them!

Often we argue for our limitations: "But I really did grow up in a dysfunctional family!" "But I really did flunk out of PE in junior high!" "Even my mom will tell you that I'm not photogenic!" As Richard Bach wrote, "Argue for your limitations and, sure enough, they're yours!" But how real are these "real" limitations?

Most of us would agree that you can't be five feet seven inches and play professional basketball. But Spud Webb is that height and played twelve seasons with the NBA, and he was the shortest person ever to win the Slam Dunk contest. Can a double amputee climb Mt. Everest? New Zealander Mark Inglis was able to do it, some twenty years after both of his legs had been amputated during a similar climb. Stephen Hawking, a quadriplegic who can only speak through a voice synthesizer, is a brilliant theoretical physicist, author, and university professor. Oprah Winfrey, born into poverty and sexually molested as a child, is one of the wealthiest and most influential people in today's world.

So were the limitations of these people really real? Most of us would say so. Yet something was more powerful than their real limitations, and I would argue that it wasn't their talent, strength, intelligence, or luck. That powerful something was the hardwiring of their brains, the conditioned beliefs they held that allowed them to break through these real limitations.

Your Conditioning: A Ferocious Warrior

It is extremely difficult to get yourself to do or be something that is counter to your conditioned beliefs. This is both the good and the bad news. It's the good news because once you have rewired your brain with beliefs that support what you desire, you'll have all of the incredible power of your brain working for you, and it will be extremely difficult to fail! The bad news is that as long as your brain is wired with the negative, limiting conditioning that has held you back, you're fighting an uphill battle against your own physiology.

> Success is often achieved by those who don't know that failure is inevitable.
>
> —*Coco Chanel*

The Problem with Affirmations

Remember that song from the musical version of *Peter Pan*? The children are encouraged to "just think lovely thoughts" in order to fly. Though "just think lovely thoughts" worked on stage (with the assistance of hidden wires), few of us who have tried to lose weight or stop bad habits by thinking lovely thoughts have much success. Why? If you've spent forty years of your life thinking of yourself as a dismal failure, simply announcing that "I'm terrific and successful in all I do!" won't cut it. It's like spraying a stinky bathroom with air freshener: the stink is still there and the combination is almost worse! That happy, fluffy thought sounds good, but the grimy, nasty belief is much stronger and more convincing. As you say "terrific and successful," your entire physiology continues to experience and react to "loser!"

EXERCISE: **Test Your Conditioning**

Try this out with one of your own limiting beliefs. Pick something negative that you say about yourself: I'm too short. I'm too old. I'm not very
smart. Other people have more talent than I have. Choose one that seems
painfully true to you. Now create an opposite statement: I'm just the right
height. I'm the perfect age. I have plenty of intelligence. I'm as talented
as the next guy. Say your positive statement out loud at least twenty times
in a row.

So, are you convinced now that your positive statement is true? Do you
feel fully capable of taking the actions that your negative belief prevented
you from taking in the past? Or do you still feel the discouragement, resistance, or fear that you felt before? Do you still hear the voice of your limiting belief arguing against the validity of your affirmative statement, giving
you proof to support its claim?

I am not saying that there is no power in affirmations. There is a way to
make them effective. But to do so, you need to cleanse or at least soften the
negative conditioned belief that runs counter to the affirmation. We'll delve
into that process in Chapter 7.

Limitations of Willpower

Often we chide ourselves for our inability to change: If I just had more
strength of character! If I just had more willpower! Full of enthusiasm and
determination, we embark on a new exercise program and healthy-eating
regime—only to find ourselves sprawled on the couch inhaling a dozen
HoHos two months later.

Willpower is a stronger, more determined voice than an affirmation. But
it still has to contend with the deep-seated conditioned belief that is resis-
tant to change. Trying to overcome a conditioned belief with willpower is
like trying to keep an inflated beach ball submerged in a swimming pool.
As soon as you release your grip on it, it pops right back up. When you

try to make a change in your life by toughing it out via willpower, the dynamic is the same: as long as willpower remains vigilant, the limiting belief stays submerged. But as soon as your willpower relaxes its grip, that limiting belief pops back to the surface and back into control.

> Those who are afraid to take the next step will have wasted their entire previous journey.
>
> —*Baron von Richthofen*

This is the dynamic that plagues those infamous yo-yo dieters: As long as the dieter remains vigilant and determined, he or she loses weight. But willpower can be exhausting, so we often relax that tense grip of willpower as soon as our weight goal has been met. And when we do, our negative conditioned belief resurfaces and takes over: *I've always been a little chubby. People are more comfortable around me if I'm fluffy, not skinny. Food is comforting, a reward after a hard day. Some of us*

EXERCISE: Finding the *Why*

Write a list of things you would like to change in your life. Some people find that it helps to organize desires into a few categories: Health, Relationships, Career, Finances, Spirituality. Include everything on this list, large or small, without censoring.

Next, pick out a few desires that feel particularly important or maybe urgent. Write each of those on a separate list, describing why that goal or desire is critical to you. Get to the heart of it. For instance, you may have the desire to begin an exercise program because you want to reduce your blood pressure. But why do you want to reduce your blood pressure? Is it so you can be around to watch your kids grow up? So you can finish that book you've always wanted to write? So you can climb Mt. Everest? Dig into your motives until you find a reason that is really compelling to you. (Hint: If you can't find a compelling reason, the odds of actually attaining that desire are slim to none!)

Finally, find a place to post this list so that you see it daily. Some clients print three by five inch cards and post them on their bathroom mirrors. Others make their list into a screensaver. Some attach their lists to areas that relate to their goals, for instance, on their refrigerator doors, on their telephones, or in their checkbooks.

> ### EXERCISE: **Teaming Up with Cheerleaders**
>
> One of the most effective aspects of any program of change is enlisting others to help you hold the course. You see this in everything from the Twelve Step programs to friends and family who cheer marathoners along the course. Find someone or a few people who will support you as you work with these processes. You might even invoke the buddy system and do the exercises together. However you arrange it, the idea is to set up a regular check-in system so that your cheerleader can help hold you accountable and cheer your progress along the way. And it's your cheerleader's job to take the other side when your old negative conditioning pops up to tell you how impossible your vision is.
>
> Who can be your cheerleader? Just about anyone. But it must be someone you trust, whom you feel comfortable with, and who believes in you and your dream. Clearly, you don't want to choose your most cynical friend or someone who might be threatened by your success!

just aren't made to be slim. Unless willpower grits its teeth and reasserts itself, the behavior that made us pudgy shows up with all 31 flavors!

And it isn't just in thoughts that the dieter's conditioned belief pops back up. It's in the taste buds and visual perception: foods that add weight will tend to taste better and look more attractive than those that don't. It's in the cravings: rather than craving fresh, crisp salad, the body will yearn for double layer, triple-chocolate fudge cake. It's in the emotions: eating will bring a sense of calm, while not eating will create a sense of anxiety. No wonder willpower feels like such a struggle!

> Right now you are one choice away from a new beginning—one that leads you toward becoming the fullest human being you can be.
>
> —*Oprah Winfrey*

The Bridge over the Chasm

If you can't fight 'em, join 'em! The path to lasting change is to work with the brain's physiology, to rewire it so it will support the changes you seek. Doesn't it make sense that you would want

EXERCISE: **Make Me a Deal**

Just about all of us are willing to do something, even if it's a bit difficult, when we know it is only for a limited time. For instance housecleaning: Imagine that I asked you to clean your entire house, top to bottom. Most of us groan and ache at the mere thought! But what if I asked you to spend just fifteen minutes each day doing a little cleaning? That doesn't sound so bad, does it? And what if I told you that if you continue this practice for thirty days, your house would be substantially tidier and more pleasant to live in? Starting to sound pretty good, right? Most of us could find that amount of time on a regular basis no matter how busy we think we are.

Well, that's what I'm asking of you. Not that you spend fifteen minutes per day cleaning your house, but that you spend that same amount of time cleaning up your brain! I'd like you to make a deal with me that you will spend fifteen minutes per day for thirty days working with the exercises in this book and on the CD. Schedule this fifteen minutes on your calendar or in your day planner. Ink it in, do not pencil it in! Consider this daily fifteen minutes an appointment with yourself that you keep, no matter what pops up. Trust me, you'll be pleased with the result.

the most powerful muscle in your body, the control center of your entire physical system, to work for you, not against you? This does not happen instantly or overnight. But through the next several chapters, I'll show you exactly how you can recondition your brain and harness its power.

As you begin to rewire your brain, you *will* run into the chasm, resistance from your old conditioning. It may make the distance between where you are and where you want to be seem to be huge. It might appear to have obstacles that are extraordinarily difficult or impossible to overcome. These are the invisible bars that seemed so very real to Mohini. So before you have rewired your brain with more positive, life-affirming beliefs, use the following exercises to keep you moving forward when that resistance from your old conditioning rears its ugly head.

Chapter 2

Your Brain: A Primer

Hopefully, I've convinced you that you need to work *with* your brain and your conditioned beliefs to create the lasting change you desire. To do so, you don't need to spend years studying the brain's physiology or spend hours staying current with all the latest research in neuroscience. But you do need to understand a few basics.

Working with the System

Imagine moving into a new home that has an automatic sprinkler system for its yard. The system turns on and off at pre-set times and, when you first move in, you may not even be aware of its schedule. It's a very efficient, convenient system that doesn't require much thought on your part. But now imagine that the rainy season starts and your system continues to water your yard. Or imagine that you install a xeriscape that requires no water at all. If you don't know how to adjust that automatic sprinkler system, suddenly this convenient system is extremely inconvenient! But you don't need to know precisely how that automatic sprinkler system does what it does. You just need a few basic instructions to adjust your system so that it is once again a help, not a hindrance.

So it is with the brain. As operators, we don't need too many details of *why* or *how* it works as it does. But we do need to know enough about its functioning so that we can focus it consciously and get it to move in the directions we desire. Specifically, we need to understand about conditioning: what it is and what it does, how it takes place unconsciously, and how to consciously reprogram unwanted conditioning toward what we desire.

What is conditioning? It's the powerful mechanism that runs your life. Neuroscience has discovered that repeated thoughts or behaviors actually form physical neuropathways in your brain. And if thoughts or patterns are repeated very often and over long periods of time, especially if they are accompanied by emotion, even stronger neuropathways are carved. When these neuropathways are in place, your brain naturally defaults to them and follows their course. Imagine ruts in a country road: As years pass, those ruts become deeper and deeper. And the deeper the rut, the more likely it is that your wheels will follow them.

So when you think a thought over and over—whether it's "I'm too dumb to do that" or "I'm brilliant, gorgeous, and capable"—it isn't just a fleeting thought. That specific persistent thought has carved out a neuropathway in your brain and is hardwired into your physiology. This is *conditioning*, the *physical* hardwiring of your brain. You may not even be aware that a thought or attitude exists—yet because it is hardwired in, it causes you to act and react in ways that validate it. Your entire system—muscles, glands, blood flow, breathing—respond to the signals from your brain based on this conditioning. That conditioned thought has you in its grip.

The fact that your brain often operates via these conditioned neuropathways isn't necessarily bad. It's actually a very efficient use of your brain power. Rather than recalculating how to fold your T-shirt, how close you should stand next to someone during conversation, or which side of the

> Neuro-plasticity is a two-way street—it can be positive or negative. We can optimize the brain's functioning by working with it to focus and remain alert—producing powerful changes that make life more fulfilling and make us feel more alive—and yet we can also decrease its functioning when we continue to focus on negativity or problems.
>
> —*Michael Merzenich, Ph.D., PBS Brain Fitness Program*

road to drive on, your brain efficiently slips into the default pathways that were carved previously. The problem comes when your conditioning is running your entire life, causing you to act and respond in ways that are counter to your desires.

Neuroscientists can view activity in the brain that represents these neuropathways using functional magnetic resonance imaging (fMRI). Without an fMRI scanner, we can't observe the functioning of our brain and the nature of our own conditioned neuropathways. But we have clear indications of when they are in place.

Automatic Pilot

A conditioned response or belief feels automatic. Think about brushing your teeth. By the time we are five or six, few of us have to really concentrate to perform the task. We brush our teeth on automatic pilot, using the same motions in the same sequence that we've always used. But when we were learning the skill as young children, we had to concentrate and figure it out: *Okay, it works better if I hold my toothbrush in my left hand and squeeze the paste with my right hand. Then transfer the brush to my right, turn on the water with my left.* However you brush your teeth, there are a hundred small motions and tiny decisions involved. But after several years, your brain simply defaults to the neuropathway you've unknowingly carved. You don't even think about it. Your brain is free to consider other matters.

University of Rochester researchers ran five psychological experiments to test how color, specifically the color red, affects men's perception of women. In one test, subjects were shown a picture of a woman with either a red border or a white border. In another, a woman's shirt in a photo was digitalized to be either red or blue. The results showed that wearing or being framed in the color red did not change subjects' ratings of the woman's likability, intelligence, or kindness. However, the woman in red was rated significantly higher in attractiveness and sexual desirability than those in other colors. And subjects reported that they would spend considerably more on a date with her! (Andrew Elliot and Daniela Niesta, "Romantic Red: Red Enhances Men's Attraction to Women," *Journal of Personality and Social Psychology,* Vol. 95, No. 5, 2008: 1150-1164)

How about driving to work? Hopefully you give this task a little more attention than teeth brushing! But if you've been employed in the same place for a while, odds are good that you can navigate your way there with little focus. In fact during your morning commute, your brain is able to move on to other tasks like creating grocery shopping lists, having imaginary arguments with your spouse, planning your day. Your brain (if not too distracted by that imaginary argument!) continues to move your eyes to observe the traffic, flex your foot on the gas pedal, hit the brake, take the right turn into the parking lot, et cetera. Rather than using all of its resources to drive you to work, your brain leaves the driving to those deeply carved neuropathways.

By the way, have you ever done something for the very first time with the feeling that you were on automatic pilot? Probably not. A new experience has no neuropathways associated with it, so you are conscious of the thinking, figuring, adjusting, and calculating that takes place.

Think of some physical sport or hobby that you've done for many years, like tennis or gardening or running. Imagine doing this and notice how it feels. You may have some thinking associated with it, but for the most part, the motions of this familiar activity probably feel pretty automatic. Now imagine doing something you've never done before, like surfing or woodworking or salsa dancing. Can you sense how much conscious awareness you would need to figure out how your body would need to move in those new activities? Your brain has not yet been conditioned to handle this unfamiliar situation.

Being on automatic pilot may be benign—or may not. You may "automatically" overspend during the holidays then wonder how your credit balances got so high. You may "automatically" find yourself late for every appointment you ever schedule. You may go on automatic pilot in romantic relationships and find yourself involved with the same user/abuser who happens to have a different name than the last one. These automatic responses are not ones you consciously prefer, and they indicate that there is a conditioned pattern running the show.

In the following exercise and others in this chapter, you'll start identifying your own conditioning. Keep in mind that much of your conditioning is benign or even positive. We'll look at some of that to help you become conscious of how much of your life is determined by conditioned responses. But clearly, not all of your conditioning needs to be changed.

Different Feels Strange

Another way to spot a conditioned behavior or thought is when a behavior or thought feels *right* to you—and its opposite behavior or thought seems strange.

Take the example of walking into a crowded elevator. What is the first thing you do when you enter an elevator? You turn around and face the doors, right? You may be able to come up with a dozen rationales for doing this (ready to exit through the doors, don't want to breathe germs on people, watching the numbers to see when I've arrived at my floor). But the truth is that you turn around without giving it any thought. It just feels right.

Now use your imagination to sense how it would feel to enter that elevator and stay facing the crowd. It feels weird, doesn't it? Maybe awkward and uncomfortable. You might feel embarrassed or even a little panicked. Your entire physiology has been conditioned to turn toward the doors. If you act counter to that conditioning, your brain sends out a panic message to your body: your heart may race, your palms may get sweaty, your face may become flushed. Rationally, you may know that there is nothing wrong or

EXERCISE: **Benign Conditioning on Automatic Pilot**

Take a few minutes to list some of your habitual patterns that are not necessarily good or bad. I've listed a few questions to get you started:

- What side of the bed do you sleep on?
- Which pant leg do you step into first?
- What is your route in the supermarket (clockwise, counter clockwise)?
- What is the first thing you do when you get out of bed in the morning?
- What is the last thing you do before you go to bed?
- When the phone rings, do you always answer it?
- Do you put on one shoe and tie it then put on the other shoe? Or do you put on both shoes then tie them?
- How do you fold your underwear?

Pay attention to all of the habitual actions you take during your daily routine. For each small, innocuous habit you identify, write down your really good rationales for why you do them as you do them. Now using this list, try modifying your behavior to do it differently. Sleep on the other side of the bed or brush your teeth first thing in the morning rather than taking a sip of water. Put your socks on before your slacks or pour milk in your bowl before the cereal. How does it feel? Odd? You may not feel much at all or you may find that even modifying a seemingly unimportant pattern feels very strange!

life-threatening about facing the crowd in the elevator rather than facing the elevator doors. But your physiology says otherwise.

> Your assumptions are your windows on the world. Scrub them off every once in a while, or the light won't come in.
>
> —*Alan Alda*

Take another example: periods of silence during conversation. Few people are perfectly comfortable in allowing a conversation to lapse and fall completely silent. We'll work pretty hard to find something to say to avoid that awkward pause, especially with people we don't know well. Why? Rationally, we know that conversational silence isn't harmful to our health. But imagine chatting with an acquaintance at a gathering, then allowing the conversation to die while you remain looking at him or her. Wouldn't that feel just plain wrong? Gawky? Disconcerting? By the way, all great salesmen know about the power of silence and how awkward we feel with it. During a sales presentation, after the closing statement has been made, the cardinal rule is that the next person who speaks, loses!

We may not care about modifying the neuropathways that make us turn around in elevators or keep us blabbering to avoid a lag in conversation. But what about how uncomfortable it feels to talk to that really attractive man or woman you've been interested in? How about that guilt you feel for not eating everything on your plate, even though you're full? What about that uneasy feeling you get when you try to balance your life and work less than sixty hours per week? Those are your clues that your brain has been conditioned to support a certain belief and align your physiology with that belief.

Mental/Emotional Treadmill

A conditioned thought often feels as if it has a life and energy of its own, as if *it's* thinking *you* rather than *you* thinking *it*. You hear a voice chattering in your head that you know is not constructive—but you can't seem to turn it off! This voice is usually quite adamant and persuasive with all sorts of

EXERCISE: It Just Feels Right

Now let's explore some of those conditioned reactions that feel so right to us. Take for instance, your response to someone who has a problem: Do you rush to come up with solutions? Do you step back to avoid getting involved? Do you listen as the other person works through it? Do you feel protective, anxious, uncomfortable, unattached?

Note that none of these actions or reactions is right or wrong. Each of us has been wired differently for this situation. The conditioned pattern you currently have may serve you very well—or it may not. But the point is to become aware of what has been unconscious. Use the following questions to unearth your own patterns, remembering that there are no correct answers:

- When you don't know what is happening, do you tend to worry or assume the best?

- When anticipating an event, do you tone down your expectations or expect a terrific outcome?

- How do you respond when given a compliment?

- When conflict happens at work or in a relationship, what is your first response?

- What is your reaction when you don't understand something?

- When problems arise, do you assume that you, someone else, or no one is at fault?

Note your responses and also how it feels to respond that way, for example: "I make a joke about the compliment and feel awkward that the attention is on me." Next, write down your very clear rationale for each of your answers: "If I don't anticipate great things, I am never disappointed." "If I ask questions, I'll appear stupid. Better to wait and figure it out."
Next, imagine someone who responds differently than you typically do. Describe that response and how it might feel to him or her. Now explain the very good rationale behind this different response. Can you make it sound as valid as the rationale behind your own normal pattern?

supporting evidence: "It's no use applying for that position. They always give it to someone who has more experience than I have. And I don't interview well anyway. They always ask tough questions, and I'm just not good on my feet. Remember that debate in the seventh grade? I was awful! I'm sure everyone was laughing at me." Have you ever found yourself arguing with a voice like that—and wondering who you were arguing with?

Or you may not hear what that conditioned thought says specifically—but you can't seem to control the behaviors and reactions it creates. For instance, you feel terrified whenever you have to speak in front of a group. You avoid strong, influential people who could help your business because you feel so intimidated by them. You always feel depressed when you pay bills, even if you have sufficient funds. You feel guilty or antsy when you are not working or doing something productive. You feel anxious when you walk into your annual check-up and have to step up on the scale. Or, you get completely tongue-tied whenever you try talking to your children about sex or the contents of your will.

These knee-jerk reactions or incessant internal voices point to the twelve by twelve-foot cages we've unconsciously built. Like a nonstop mental treadmill, they are the thoughts and attitudes that will not let us off. Once a negative attitude or fear is hardwired in, not even the most brilliant logic or reasoning will convince us out of it, and no amount of effort will offset reactions and behaviors it causes. We're like the Borg in *Star Trek*, moving and reacting according to the signals in our brains. The point then is to rewire those signals so that we are moving and reacting in ways that are positive.

Who Dunnit?

Many clients ask me how these conditioned patterns, especially the negative ones, started in the first place. Were our parents to blame? Our culture? Television ads? That mean old first-grade teacher with the scary voice? Did

> The good thing about the past is that it is over.
>
> —*Richard Bandler*

it happen because of one traumatic event or over years? Could I have responded in a different way back then? Is it an inclination of my genetic make-up, or was I raised to follow this pattern?

The truth is that it doesn't matter. Whoever, whenever, however your conditioning took hold, it is active in your present. And it is in the present that you can work to modify your conditioning. In some cases, identifying the original cause or source of a limiting conditioned belief can be helpful. But too often, we get stuck there, dissecting once again how Aunt Agnes traumatized us by criticizing our penmanship in grade school. We can't rearrange the past or erase the fact that unwanted beliefs were somehow carved into our brains. But we definitely can take charge and rewire those beliefs now.

That said, two sources of conditioning are extremely powerful: experiences of early childhood and our culture.

Early Childhood

As children, we are open, vulnerable, and innocent. We drink in our environments without filters or preconceptions, absorbing experiences like thirsty sponges. We take it all in at face value, literally, as gospel, like computers that lack virus protection.

A friend shared a story from her early childhood when she visited the zoo with her mom, along with a friend from kindergarten and his mom. When my friend had to use the restroom, her mom got directions from a guard, which led them through the snake pavilion. They happened to walk past a python's cage as it was being fed lunch: a live rat. My friend's mother shrieked, covered her eyes, and rushed them away from the scene. Her mom yelled at the guard who had directed them there and generally created a scene that left my friend embarrassed and shaken.

But the other mom stayed at the snake's cage with her son. She explained to him that this is how nature works, that we all live within a cycle of life. She talked about the wonder of wildlife, all the things we had yet to discover, and the importance of protecting the world and its creatures.

Would you be surprised to learn that my friend grew up to be a vegetarian, terrified of snakes, spiders, rodents, and animals in general? While her kindergarten friend has become a zoologist who lives and works on a wildlife reserve in Kenya?

Cultural Conditioning

Conditioned beliefs that have broad cultural agreement, like racism, sexism, or ageism, can be difficult to pinpoint. We are surrounded by subtle and not-so-subtle messages that support these cultural beliefs, making them implicitly "true." Our *conscious thoughts* may be politically correct, but our *feelings* reveal the stronger conditioned belief underneath. For instance, those of us in the United States may be very clear that not all Muslims are terrorists, yet get nervous when we board an airplane with several men in turbans. Often we can monitor ourselves and make sure that our *actions* reflect our conscious choices, not our knee-jerk reactions or *feelings*. But

Harvard scientists Anthony G. Greenwals, Mahzarin Banaji, and Brian Nosek developed a tool to measure the subconscious conditioning that colors our observations. Using the Implicit Association Test (IAT), the team is able to observe how we automatically connect certain groups of people with certain adjectives—despite *conscious* beliefs that argue against these connections. Of people who reported having no bias prior to taking the IAT, over 80 percent showed unconscious negative attitudes toward the elderly; 75–80 percent of Caucasians and Asians tested as having unconscious pro-white associations compared to their less positive associations with African Americans. To take the test yourself and unearth some of your own cultural conditioning, go to www.implicit.harvard.edu.

unearthing those unconscious conditioned beliefs and working to change them is always more reliable in the long run.

The course of history can also modify our conditioned beliefs. For over two hundred years, the United States has been plagued by the invisible bars of racism. Despite our *conscious* beliefs, the emphasis on politically correct language, and decades of equal opportunity laws on the books, the unconscious underlying conditioning of many Americans continued to view—and *treat*—non-Caucasians as lesser. But in 2008, Barack Obama became the first African American to be elected as president of the United States. Will this historic election erase racism completely? No. Those underlying conditioned beliefs still reside in many of us. But the election did mark a

EXERCISE: Tackling the Boogie Man

In this exercise, you'll begin to identify the conditioned beliefs, the specific hardwiring, that has been blocking your efforts to reach your goals and desires. As long as these limiting beliefs remain unconscious, they maintain the power to sabotage your efforts. Once they are brought to light of day, you can work with them using processes I'll show you in the next chapters.

Begin by listing goals and desires that you identified in Chapter 1 and any others that may occur to you.

For each goal or desire, write about the efforts you have made in the past to achieve them and the results of those efforts.

Next, list all the limiting beliefs you have about each goal. Remember that your limiting beliefs may sound very true to you: "I can't find a relationship because all the good men are taken." "I can't start that career because I'm too old."

If you can't identify what the limiting belief says, how does it feel? To get to that feeling, imagine taking action toward your goal or remember actions you've taken in the past. Did staying on a diet feel difficult? Discouraging? As if you were depriving yourself of pleasure? Note those feelings. Often as you experience those feelings, the negative belief associated with them will surface.

shift in our culture, and today's young children will *never* question whether a person of color is qualified to be elected to our country's highest office. For them, it will be a given.

> We are betrayed by what is false within.
>
> —*George Meredith*

To work with our conditioning, we don't need to spend time peeling back the layers and scrutinizing the where, when, who, and why of it. Our conditioning is here and active in us in this moment so we can deal with it here and now. But without overanalyzing it, sometimes it can be helpful to recall an earlier event that triggered a conditioned response or to identify cultural signals that support unwanted reactions.

Through the exercises, you are beginning to identify the limiting beliefs that your brain is working as hard as it can to support! If you believe that you are "not good with numbers," sure enough, your brain will scramble your vision and blur your analytical process so that financial statements look indecipherable. If your conditioning says that "success requires sacrifice," your brain will make sure that you feel anxious when it catches you working less than a sixty-hour work week. If your brain is convinced that you are "too old to find romance," you'll be blind to attractive people who might be interested in you. But for each of these scenarios, I have to question your seemingly true limiting belief. Because somewhere there is an individual who flunked out of math but has mastered financial statements, another who is successful *and* lives a balanced life, and another who is older and less attractive than you but has a fun romantic life.

It may initially seem discouraging to view your list of limiting beliefs. But if your brain can support those limiting beliefs so powerfully, imagine what it can do when you've rewired it with beliefs that are aligned with what you desire! Conditioning can work for or against you. *You can use conditioning consciously, or you can let it use you unconsciously.* As brain scientists probe the limits of neuroplasticity, they have discovered that the brain can *change* physically as a result of the thoughts we think. So we have

> What we must try to be, of course, is ourselves and wholeheartedly. We must find out what we really are and what we really want.
>
> —*Nelson Boswell*

the capacity to rewire the brain with new neuro-pathways, new thoughts and attitudes that can remove our cage and free the Mohini within!

Chapter 3

The Creator of Your Reality

The Most Powerful Truth

The most powerful truth I know is that, consciously or unconsciously, we each create our own experience. I'm guessing that you have heard this before from motivational speakers, spiritual leaders, philosophers, and metaphysicians. "You create your own reality." "You attract into your life what you believe you deserve." "Life is what you make of it." Many people accept this concept as true on some level. But how many of us actually *experience* it? That the life we are living daily is truly our own creation? Far, far fewer.

Underneath, I think most of us feel that external circumstance has a major impact on the lives we lead. We may feel that we are unfortunate victims of circumstance, fighting an uphill battle to get where we want to be. Or we may feel that circumstance is benign, yet still see external factors as out-

29

> If you are distressed by anything external, the pain is not due to the thing itself but to your own estimate of it; and this you have the power to revoke at any moment.
>
> —*Marcus Aurelius*

side of our control and playing a critical role in shaping who we are and what we can expect from life. Even in theory, it's hard to grasp that the life we are living is totally of our making and that even outside factors have been created by or attracted to us based on what we believe and think about. But if you can truly grasp that only *you create*—or more accurately, your conditioning creates—*your reality,* you've got the most important key to lasting personal transformation.

If you learn nothing else from this book, that experiential knowing alone would completely transform your life. So let me restate it: Our feelings and reactions are *not* caused by external events or circumstance. Reactions and feelings are internally generated by the beliefs and stories that have been programmed into us. Though we may remain unconscious of our beliefs, they determine *specifically* how we react to the people, events, and situations in our life. They determine what we see and hear, how accurately we process information, and how well we perform. They determine our health, our wealth, and our happiness. These conditioned beliefs and stories create our reality, *not* external circumstance.

Wouldn't it feel amazing to really experience yourself as fully in charge of your destiny? Wouldn't you feel terrific knowing that no circumstance or external factor stands in the way of what you desire? What if you could draw to yourself the circumstances you wish?

> Reality is the leading cause of stress amongst those in touch with it.
>
> —*Jane Wagner*

Over the next pages, I'd like to convince you that this is exactly how it works—not just on a philosophical or metaphysical level but physically within your system as directed by your brain. And even though you've mainly used your reality-creating power *unconsciously* until now, you *can* use it consciously.

Your Conditioned Perception

We perceive what we expect to perceive, and our perception creates our reality. I know this statement is loaded, so let's break it down: (1) our conditioning colors our perceptions of people and events, (2) our perceptions trigger specific conditioned responses, and (3) the combination of these two creates our reality, our destiny.

First, though few of us would like to admit it, our perception of people and situations around us is not at all objective, even when we are trying to be. Within every encounter, our brain makes judgments, attends to certain details and ignores others, processes incoming information according to prior experience and context, and so on. And much of the brain's activity is guided by our conditioning, those previously carved neuropathways that reflect what we believe to be true.

> What we are seeing . . . is that happiness can be conceptualized not simply as a state or as a trait but as the product of trainable skills, skills that can be enhanced through mental training.
>
> —*Richard Davidson*

It's like looking through an antique leaded glass window. We see some of what is out there but the image is distorted, misshapen, or fuzzy in places. This is the work of our brain fulfilling its mission to support our conditioned beliefs and to make those beliefs into reality.

Our Personal Realities

Let's start with the obvious: we each view the world differently. I attended a conference recently with a couple of colleagues. One of the speakers made a remark about organized religion: "Idiots like Robertson, Falwell, and Roberts no more teach the message of Jesus Christ than bin Laden, Yassin, and Saddam Hussein represent the true message of Islam." My colleague Sandy became so angry and offended that she stomped out of the room.

> Instead of saying that man is the creature of circumstance, it would be nearer the mark to say that man is the architect of circumstance.
>
> —*Thomas Carlyle*

My other colleague, Betsy, laughed heartily at the speaker's remarks and listened to him with obvious enthusiasm.

So how is it that an external event—a comment made in a keynote speech—elicits such different reactions and feelings? We've all had such experiences: We think that a particular film is moving and insightful; our neighbor thinks the same film is trivial and maudlin. We listen to a political candidate and feel inspired and hopeful. Our coworker hears the same speech and feels manipulated and angry. We love the sound of thunder; our partner feels anxious and restless during a storm.

The truth is that our feelings and reactions are not caused by the external event itself. They are created by those conditioned beliefs carved into our brains *about* such events. And the important point is not which conditioned response is correct but whether your conditioned response, feeling, and reactions to external events *serve* you or *sabotage* you.

For instance, you may find yourself yelling at your spouse whenever he or she is late. That response is not right or wrong, but it certainly contributes to the dynamic of your relationship, creating a marital reality you may or may not want. Or you may freeze up and clam up when your boss criticizes your work. This response is not necessarily bad, but does it contribute positively to where you want to be in your career? Is there another option?

That Tree in the Forest

Remember the old koan: If a tree falls in the forest but no one is there to hear it, does it still make a sound? It isn't external circumstance that creates feelings and responses but your cognitive *awareness* of it coupled with your conditioned beliefs about it. The first time I grasped this concept on a visceral level was during high school when my maternal grandmother died. She passed away on a Saturday morning in November when I was scheduled to take my SAT exams. Our school's homecoming dance was that evening.

Not wanting to upset me before the exam or ruin my excitement about the dance, my parents decided not to tell me about my granny's death. They told me the following morning and I was instantly consumed with grief. But it struck me that, even though my favorite granny had died that previous day, all I had felt on Saturday was the nervousness of testing and the thrill of going to the dance. A major event in my life had happened but *because I was not aware of it, I had no reaction to it.* The experience of grief was generated internally by my cognitive awareness, *not* by the external event itself.

Another example: A photographer told me that he was camping at a remote lake during the events of 9/11. Because he had no knowledge of the tragedy occurring, he spent that day in utter peace and bliss, capturing tranquil photos of wild birds. It was only when he returned to the city and learned about the historic catastrophe that he felt the anguish the rest of the world experienced.

Another friend tells the story of unknowingly spending an entire day at the office with his zipper unzipped! He felt perfectly confident and composed during meetings and interactions with his staff. His embarrassment

EXERCISE: What's Going on in Your World?

If our feelings and reactions are derived only from events and circumstances we are aware of, doesn't it stand to reason that we should *choose* what to know? Think about the books you read, the shows you watch, the news you follow, the music you listen to. Though I don't recommend retreating to a cave on a mountaintop to avoid all negative input, are there some things you could cut out of your awareness diet to feel better and more empowered? Are there things you could add?

only hit when he got home and took a look in the mirror! Had he not become aware of his unzipped state, he easily could have survived this humiliating experience with no reaction at all.

Ignorance *Can* Be Bliss

My husband and I experienced another poignant example of how ignorance of external circumstances can affect feelings and behavior. We were vacationing in a friend's cabin in a remote area. The caretaker of the property was a charming young man who was very knowledgeable about the island, its ecosystems, weather patterns, and history. For the first few days, we enjoyed his company daily and he regaled us with interesting stories and fascinating facts.

But on the fourth day, this young man discovered that I am a psychologist and author, and that my husband is a psychiatrist. Immediately, our new friend became tongue-tied whenever he tried to speak to us and stuttered so badly that he could hardly complete a sentence. He stopped dropping by to visit and avoided our company. After a few days of this, my husband corralled him and discovered that this young man felt very uncomfortable around people who are educated. He had barely completed high school and was self-conscious about his lack of education.

The important point is that as long as he *did not know* that we had advanced degrees, he was perfectly comfortable with us. When he found out, his entire being was affected. Nothing at all had changed in the situation itself or in the way we interacted with him and felt about him. But knowing about our education level changed his entire perception of the situation and our friendship. And that perception fired off a conditioned response in his brain that affected his physiology, causing him to act, feel, even speak differently! The circumstance itself did not cause these reactions. The "reality" his brain perceived, that he was not smart enough to converse with us, was the culprit. His conditioning colored his percep-

EXERCISE: **What Don't I Know?**

This exercise is a good one for shaking up your normal response patterns. As you interact with others during the day, assume that there is something you don't know about the situation and make up a story about what that unknown information might be. For instance, when someone cuts you off in traffic, you might think, "He's headed to the hospital with his very ill wife." Or if a coworker does something nice for you, "He's just trying to get on my good side so I'll cover for him later." As you play this game, you'll notice that you can come up with a variety of reasonable alternative background scenarios, especially regarding someone else's motivations. Notice also how differently you perceive and feel about the situation based on the back story you tell yourself.

tion, which triggered his programming and its conditioned reactions and feeling.

Can you relate? Have you ever met someone for the first time and enjoyed a pleasant interaction, only to find out something about that person that throws you off balance? She's been convicted of a felony; he's got thirteen children; she's got an incurable disease; he's going to be your new boss! Suddenly, the situation seems different. An interaction that was very comfortable may no longer be so. Your conditioning leaps in to respond to this new information and casts a totally new light on what is happening. Words are heard differently; facial expressions and body language are reinterpreted. Your personal reality of this interaction has changed, not by the new information itself, but by your conditioned response to it.

> I am a kind of paranoid in reverse. I suspect people of plotting to make me happy.
>
> —*J. D. Salinger*

You See and Hear What You Expect

In the book *Blink*, Malcolm Gladwell cites a good example of "you see what you believe" from the world of classical music. Until a few decades ago, very few women were ever hired to play in classical orchestras, especially in Europe and _especially_ in horn sections. The seemingly reasonable rationale behind this lack of female hires was that women had different lip structures and smaller hands, and were generally physically weaker with less lung capacity. When women auditioned, conductors and committees actually heard how these physical differences affected women's performance: shortness of breath, lack of power and resonance, inability to sustain notes, and inferior quality.

But a few decades ago, orchestras began using screens during auditions so that the musicians auditioning could not be seen. Judging committees also assigned performers numbers rather than names so they could not be identified. Within thirty years of instituting those practices, the number of women hired to play for top-tier orchestras increased fivefold!

Was the prior discrimination against women pure prejudice? Probably not. The judges were most likely very sincere about wanting the best musicians for their orchestras. It is more likely that conductors and committees _truly believed_ that feminine physical characteristics resulted in lesser performance. When they auditioned female performers, these judges fell into that conditioned belief and their brains made sure this "truth" was supported: breathiness was perceived, tones sounded less resonant and weaker. The bias against female performers was not just a thought. It affected the judges' entire physiology so that they _heard_ what they expected to hear.

But with the screen in place, the judges did not see male or female. Their brains had no conditioned belief to support. Perception could be objective, based more purely on the sound of the music itself. The result? Female musicians were judged to be as adept or even more adept than their male counterparts.

This dynamic of perceiving through our conditioned beliefs is common to all of us. Our brains make sure that we see and hear what we expect to see and hear. If you believe that your sister has always been critical of you, every word she says will sound judgmental. Every action she takes will feel adversarial. Every facial expression will look disapproving. When you interact with her, your physiology will move into defense mode: clenched jaw, churning stomach, tense neck and shoulders.

"But, you don't understand! She really *is* critical of me!" Perhaps. But what if those same words, actions, and facial expressions came from your very best friend who absolutely worships you? Would you perceive them the same way? Can you feel how that strong belief about your sister would affect what you perceive? How it changes your reality of the situation? Can you sense how your entire physiology would respond? That reaction is your brain doing its very best to make sure your conditioned belief is made *real*.

Making a Lie True

In seminars, I run attendees through an exercise so they can experience for themselves how their brains will help them see what they believe or expect to see. We show two side-by-side video clips of the same man speaking into the camera, but the sound has been muted. I tell participants that in one of the clips, the man is lying and in the other, he is telling the truth. I give them a few minutes to study his body language and determine which is which. Invariably, the audience comes up with very strong opinions about the clips. They point to "squinty eyes" in one or "agitated eyebrows" in the other. They clearly see defensiveness in his posture or shallow breathing.

Then I reveal that the guy wasn't lying in either clip—he was reciting a poem, the same poem in fact. But based on *false* information, the audience still found evidence. Their brains went to work to *perceive* something that was not there.

> There has been much tragedy in my life; at least half of it has actually happened.
>
> —*Mark Twain*

A colleague, Helen, had a similar *ah-ha!* moment. Helen used to attend a company-sponsored aerobics class during her lunch hour, and her

> It ain't so much the things you don't know that get you into trouble. It's the things you know that just ain't so.
>
> —*Artemus Ward*

classmates regularly threw surprise birthday parties for one another. Because Helen had a work meeting on her birthday, she knew she wouldn't be at aerobics. So she asked Danny, who was also in the class, to let everyone know she couldn't be at aerobics that day so they wouldn't go to the trouble of bringing cake and refreshments.

Later on the day of her birthday, Helen ran into Danny. "You missed a great party," he said. "What? You didn't tell the class I couldn't come?" "No, I forgot. Everyone wondered why you didn't show for it." Furious, Helen stormed out of the office. She remembered seeing large boxes in the break room and realized that those must have been the refreshments and cake for the party she hadn't attended. She thought about the classmate she'd run into in the elevator and how tersely she had spoken to Helen. Over the next hour, Helen's emotions ranged from anger at Danny to worry about her classmate's upset to sadness for missing her own party. When Helen finally calmed down and accepted the situation, she returned to the office and apologized to Danny—who promptly laughed out loud. "I was just pulling your chain! I told everybody last week. There was no party!"

Moral of the story? Helen had experienced an hour of intense emotions based on something that never happened—something she only believed happened. Her brain had helped her find evidence to support her belief (packages in the break room, her elevator encounter with the classmate). The entire episode was based on a delusion—but Helen's brain made sure that it felt, looked, and sounded totally genuine. It manufactured facts and emotion to create her reality.

If a brain can do this so completely with a new belief (i.e., that a party had taken place), how much more powerfully do you think it operates to manufacture reality to support those conditioned beliefs that have been carved deeply into it over many years?

Looking in the Looking Glass

In his groundbreaking book written in 1960, *Psycho-Cybernetics*, Dr. Maxwell Maltz, a prominent plastic surgeon, writes of the inability of his patients to see themselves as others saw them. A young man who had surgery to minimize his very large ears still saw huge ears after surgery had successfully reduced them to normal size. A drop-dead gorgeous woman by anyone's standards continued to be self-conscious of her "homeliness" despite all efforts to reassure her. When Dr. Maltz asked his patients to draw portraits of themselves, they more often than not still drew in the feature that had been surgically corrected *as if nothing had changed.* Dr.

> We do not believe in ourselves until someone reveals that deep inside us is valuable, worth listening to, worthy of our trust, sacred to our touch. Once we believe in ourselves we can risk curiosity, wonder, spontaneous delight or any experience that reveals the human spirit.
>
> —*e. e. cummings*

EXERCISE: **What Do You Expect?**

Make a list of some of your expectations, both positive and negative. Your list should include yourself ("I'll never be good at math." "I'm a great housekeeper."), other individuals ("My brother has always been talented." "My boss is always out to get me.") and groups ("All politicians are crooks." "Women are such good listeners."). Keep in mind that your strongest expectations, your most deep-seated conditioned beliefs, will sound absolutely, undeniably true to you. You will undoubtedly have plenty of evidence to support them!

Now, taking your list of expectations one by one, imagine that each one is based on a delusion, misconception, or false information. How would that feel? How would your experience of yourself change? How would you react differently in interactions with that other person or those people? What might you see differently or interpret differently?

And the most important question: Does your original expectation, your conditioned belief, *serve* you or work *against* you?

> Real difficulties can be overcome; it is only the imaginary ones that are unconquerable.
>
> — *Theodore N. Vail*

Maltz came to realize that many of his patients truly could *not* see themselves as anything other than the ingrained self-image they had carried for years. They expected to see large ears and homely faces in the mirror, and that's exactly what they saw.

Perception Determines What Is Possible

Perception, which is determined by your beliefs and your conditioning, also affects performance. This is demonstrated in this true story about a graduate-level mathematics student at the University of California at Berkeley in 1939, George Dantzig.

George showed up late for class one day and found two problems on the blackboard that he believed to be homework assignments. He copied the problems and took them home. George struggled to find solutions to these problems but, knowing he was as capable as any other student in the class, he worked diligently until he solved both of them two days later. Six weeks after turning them in, George was contacted by his very excited professor, Jerzy Neyman. The two problems had not been homework assignments at all. Dr. Neyman had written them on the board to show the class two of the most famous *unsolved problems in statistics*.

Yet George had been able to solve these problems. Why? Probably because he, and his brain, believed he could. Could the other students in the class have solved them as well? Perhaps. But all of the other students in class knew that the problems had never been solved. Their brains perceived a situation that was unknown and probably impossible; George's brain perceived a situation that was difficult but doable. *It was not the circumstance, but the perception of the circumstance that made the difference.* Though they did not have the technology to do so at that time, wouldn't it have been fascinating to see the activity in George's brain versus that of his classmates when viewing those problems?

Our conditioned beliefs often determine what is possible. Think of the story of the four-minute mile. For decades, runners had tried to run a mile in under four minutes. Roger Bannister finally accomplished this feat in 1954. Within one year after he did, thirty-seven other runners did the same. Within two years, more than three hundred runners had broken the four-minute mile! So what had changed? There was no new technology in shoes or evolutionary improvement in the human body that made this possible. The one thing that had changed within that time was the *belief* that running a mile under four minutes was possible. With that belief in place, athletes' brains applied themselves, organizing the physiology of each runner to support this possibility.

> There is only one real sin and that is to persuade oneself that the second best is anything but second best.
>
> —*Doris Lessing*

Determined to Fail

Similarly, the brain works hard to support a belief that something is impossible. Imagine a student who is convinced that she is no good at languages. It doesn't matter if "bad at languages" is a message her parents instilled or if she had an early traumatic experience with a foreign-speaking person. For whatever reason, this student is certain that she will never learn to speak in a language other than her own. What happens when she goes to French class? Her brain immediately activates all systems to support her belief. It may slow activity in the left hemisphere (where language is processed) and tone down auditory acuity. The brain, recognizing French class as a threat to her survival, will activate the anxiety response: speed up heart rate, activate shallow breathing, and pump in cortisol, the stress hormone that supports survival functions but further impairs analytical thinking.

> Life is a process of becoming, a combination of states we have to go through. Where people fail is that they wish to elect a state and remain in it. This is a kind of death.
>
> —*Anais Nin*

On the other hand, another student of similar IQ may believe that she is terrific with languages. This student walks into French class relaxed and confident because her brain recognizes the situation as positive and safe, so her body does not interfere with her learning. Her brain makes sure that the left hemisphere is dominant and that her auditory acuity is sharp. When she misses the pronunciation of a word it does not upset her because she understands that this is natural in learning a new language. This student's brain has set her up for success. Same circumstance, but two totally different perceptions of the circumstance. Perception, colored by conditioned beliefs, triggered the conditioned response, resulting in success or failure.

EXERCISE: If You Knew You Couldn't Fail . . .

Motivational speakers often use the phrase: If you knew you *could not* fail, what would you do? Let's rephrase that slightly to: If your brain was convinced and wired with the truth that you could not fail, what could you do?

Make a list of things you desire that have seemed out of reach or even impossible to you up until now. Pick out two or three that are the most inspiring to you. Next to these, rather than telling your old story of why these goals are unattainable, create some new "evidence" that points to their viability. For instance, you might reference someone who actually has done what you would like to do. Or you might recall related experiences in your past where you've achieved some success with something similar. You might note the people who might be willing to help you. This new evidence may not yet seem as convincing as your old story. But it *will* feel more persuasive when we begin to rewire your brain with a more positive conditioned belief!

Your Choice

Sometimes I get resistance from clients when I talk about the fact that their reality is personal and self-created: "But my boss really *is* a tyrant!" "My spouse really *is* cheating on me!" "I really *do* have this illness, disability, physical issue!" I concede that you may have every right to feel bad, mad, sad, and rotten. You are totally justified and every court in the land would agree with you.

> The greatest weapon against stress is our ability to choose one thought over another.
>
> —*William James*

But is that the choice you wish to make?

Though your conditioning may try to convince you otherwise, you have the power to perceive *any* situation or circumstance differently, to program in a more positive belief about it, and to react and feel differently. The circumstance may or may not change—*but your life will be transformed.*

Damage Control

It's always your choice. But you should be aware that holding onto a personal reality that is negative may be doing some serious damage to your physical system. The experience of negativity—blaming, making negative judgments, complaining, boredom, anxiousness, frustration, anger—triggers and activates the infamous stress hormone cortisol.

Cortisol, although given the label "stress hormone," also has an essential and beneficial effect on the body. There is a need for balance for everything within ourselves, even cortisol, and the body must regulate itself. Without increased cortisol levels in the morning, we would never get out of bed. In dangerous or threatening real-life situations, cortisol provides a quick surge of energy allowing us to move quickly to protect ourselves. Other results of mild bursts in cortisol levels are increased memory functioning,

A study conducted by the Touch Research Institute (University of Miami School of Medicine) evaluated the effect of a mother's psychological stress on the weight of her fetus during midgestation and prematurity, and the birth weight of the infant. The researchers evaluated ninety-eight women (an average age of twenty-six years). During a single visit, they estimated fetal weight by ultrasound; assessed maternal stress, depression, and anxiety with three self-reported questionnaires; and obtained urinary samples for analysis of cortisol levels. The results showed that elevated levels of cortisol from maternal psychological distress had significant impact on lowering the weight of the fetus and subsequently the baby at birth. (Miguel A. Diego et al., *Psychosomatic Medicine,* 68, 2006: 747–753.)

increased immune functioning, and higher pain tolerance. All of these effects reflect the body's survival mechanism in response to stressful life situations.

The danger to our body comes with *increased* and *prolonged* release of cortisol—when we are unable to switch off the perception of threat and thus are unable to switch from the stress response to the relaxation response. When we live under constant stress, our body becomes unable to regulate itself. We become excitable, edgy, and irritable. With excessive amounts of cortisol flowing through our veins, our whole body is affected and impaired. With our mental focus on survival, our analytical ability is blocked, and we are less able to think clearly and make good decisions. We may become accident-prone. Our energy is impaired and reduced, negative emotions become more frequent and erratic, and we are less effective in managing our emotions. With prolonged stress, high cortisol levels decrease bone density resulting in vulnerability to fractures and breaks. Heart rate

> We can let the circumstances of our lives harden us so that we become increasingly resentful and afraid, or we can let them soften us, and make us kinder. We always have the choice.
>
> —*the Dalai Lama*

and blood pressure is increased; our metabolism is impaired, resulting in increased abdominal fat, which is associated with heart problems. The regulation of blood sugars is impaired, resulting in weakness. In some, seizures and coma may occur.

In other words, the personal reality you are creating for yourself may very well kill you. Your choice.

Chapter 4

Power of Feelings

The words *feelings* and *emotions* are often used interchangeably, but they are *not* the same. When I started my work many years ago, I realized that it is critical for us to make a clear distinction between feelings and emotions, not just in theory but within our day-to-day experience. Both are sensed in the body and cause physiological responses, and the process to rewire the brain works with both feelings and emotions—but in different ways.

On the Cellular Level

A one-celled organism—an amoeba—has *feelings*. Feelings are necessary in order for the amoeba to react to conditions sensed in the environment. Without them, the organism dies. But *emotions* are the result of our conditioning and include the stories or beliefs hardwired into our brains. They are the result of specific interpretations of our environment based on these stories and beliefs.

An amoeba responds to light per its feeling but has no stories that impact that response. It never says, "Wow, maybe I'd look better with a tan and the other amoebae will like me better. I'll stay out here just a little longer. . ." The amoeba's feeling is pure, survival-oriented, and intelligent. But multicellular beings tend to muck up this clean and efficient feeling-response process. We create multiple stories for ourselves. These stories attach to our pure feelings, turning them into not-so-pure emotions, which then become hardwired into our brains. This hardwiring causes us to react in ways that an amoeba would find pretty crazy!

Powerful Split Second

The dictionary defines *emotions* as: (1) heightened feeling or a strong feeling about somebody or something; (2) agitation or disturbance caused by strong feelings. In other words, the feeling comes first, but in our day-to-day experience, we may not even notice it. The space between a feeling turning into an emotion can be just a split second, so the feeling itself is often missed. The transition from feeling to emotion happens so quickly (and usually without conscious awareness) that we can confuse the two as the same thing. But they aren't, and that split second is the most critical, most precious point in time. It is within that microsecond that we have the choice to take charge of our behavior—or allow the emotions created by prior conditioning to rule us.

In the pure feeling cycle, feeling moves to awareness and allows appropriate choice or action. The emotional cycle, on the other hand, is more convoluted: Feeling elicits a conditioned story and its associated emotion that triggers an unconscious reaction, which in turn exacerbates emotion, which results in heighten reaction, and . . . the emotional cycle can be endless!

I know the distinction between emotion and feeling is tough to grasp, especially on the experiential level. I wrestled with it myself for quite a while. But this distinction is key to lasting change, so most of this chapter will be focused on helping you experience this distinction in your own life.

I'm Gonna Kill That Guy

Take the pretty common example of getting cut off in traffic. You're driving along and someone zooms out of nowhere and takes over your lane. The feeling is that fast rush of adrenaline and the instant physical reaction that causes you to tense slightly, grab the wheel, and swerve to avoid a collision. Like an inherently intelligent amoeba, you allow your feeling to guide your reaction.

But often an emotion develops next, and that emotion *always has a storyline*: "That idiot! What does he think he's doing? I could have been killed along with everyone else. What a jerk! They shouldn't give licenses to idiots like that." Sound familiar? When you add the story (which, by the way, is a story or belief based on your prior conditioning), you don't just feel the physiological response that helped you swerve and avoid a collision. You are now furious, blood is rushing to your head, your jaw is clenched, and your stomach is churning. You're ready to kill the guy! You are fully into the emotion of anger—but it *would not have happened without that storyline.*

By the way, notice how fast-acting and brilliant your body is in that situation. You face a real-life threat, your feelings signal your brain, which immediately sends your physiology into survival mode to execute appropriate action. And next, because you add the story that this jerk nearly killed you and is dangerous to society, your brain sends out the next signal and your whole physiology goes into full attack mode, preparing itself for battle. The guy is probably ten miles away but your body remains fully prepared to hunt him down!

> Anger is never without Reason, but seldom with a good One.
>
> —*Benjamin Franklin*

EXERCISE: **What's Your Story?**

In the last chapter, I asked you to tell a different story about common daily experiences. You were able to notice how a different story created a different "reality" and emotional perspective. For this chapter, I'd like you to become even more aware of the stories or beliefs attached to your emotions. I'd like you to acknowledge these stories and become fully aware of the emotion accompanying them.

As you go through your day, notice when an emotion pops up. Maybe you see a panhandler on the street and experience disgust or pity. A salesperson is abrupt with you, and you feel angry or demeaned. Notice and name that emotion.

Next, what is the underlying message or story associated with that emotion? It may have more than one layer. "That person should just get a job and stop living off of others" may have another story underneath it: "If I see that person as acceptable, maybe I'll end up just like him!"

Without judging yourself or being politically correct, allow your underlying story to reveal itself. Stay with the emotion, noticing where it resides in your body and how it feels. Often just this step of acknowledging an emotion and its story will release its hold on you.

What about Love?

Love, especially romantic love, has often been compared to a form of insanity. But does it start that way? Remember when you first met someone special? You felt an instant attraction and a wonderful sense of appreciation and caring. In those first moments, you enjoyed that person simply for who they were right then, not based on a list of criteria you may have developed. Your appreciation was not based on what they could potentially do or be for you.

> Speak when you are angry and you will make the best speech you will ever regret.
>
> —*Ambrose Bierce*

But very quickly, the stories begin: I love him or her *because*. . . "I love her because she is beautiful and always makes me laugh. I love her because she is sweet and caring." "I love him because he is kind and responsible.

I love him because he is strong and charming." These stories revolve around your conditioned beliefs about what makes a person lovable. And once a relationship starts, underlying beliefs about how you know if they love you back emerge as well: "I know she loves me because she always listens to me and compliments me often." "I know he loves me because he always takes care of me and is physically affectionate."

Gravity. It keeps you rooted to the ground. In space, there's not any gravity. You just kind of leave your feet and go floating around. Is that what being in love is like?

—*Josh Brand and John Falsey, Northern Exposure, "The Pilot"*

EXERCISE: How Do I Love Thee?

Love in its purest form is life's greatest blessing! However, even its purest form is usually tainted by our conditioned beliefs. In this exercise, I want you to unearth some of those beliefs about love so you can make a choice whether to keep them or rewire them.

List the people in your life you love the most. Next to each name, make notes about *why* you love them. Then for each one, explain how you know whether they love you. What do they do or say to prove it to you?

Next, considering each loved one individually, imagine that some of the lovable characteristics you listed for them disappear. For instance, the loved one who is fun may become depressed. The lover who is handsome may become disfigured. What happens to your emotion of love? Can you still feel love for them beyond the conditioned criteria you have held them to?

Finally, review the indicators you listed that prove to you when another loves you. Did you come to these indicators based on how the other expresses love, or are they based on how you (or your parents or your previous lover) express it? Is it possible that the other person loves you even without these indicators? How could you know?

The point is not that your beliefs about loving or being loved are wrong. The only question to ask about each is: Does this serve me? Does this belief make my life fuller and richer?

> I believe love is primarily a choice and only sometimes a feeling. If you want to feel love, choose to love and be patient.
>
> —*Gordon Atkinson*

These stories and beliefs spring from your brain's hardwiring, your own conditioning. Maybe these conditioned beliefs come from too many fairytales where the prince is always handsome and charming and the princess is sweet and beautiful. Maybe it comes from decisions you made as a child about your imperfect parents and their poor relationship. "If Dad had been responsible and kind, Mom wouldn't have yelled at him." "If Mom had taken better care of her looks, Dad wouldn't have ignored her." Whatever the source, the stories you start to tell about that special person have little or nothing to do with who he or she really is or how he or she really feels about you.

These conditioned stories become attached to the initial feelings that were open, innocent, story-less. They become an emotion. And what is that emotion called? Conditional love. As conditions change, supporting or contradicting your conditioned beliefs about lovable people and how you should be loved, your emotional response of love turns on and off like a spigot. In contrast, I would argue that *un*conditional love is that *feeling* sense, the one that appreciates another in each present moment without cause or judgment.

Plugged into Your Physiology

Both *feelings* and *emotions* are felt in the body. But while *feelings* can be subtle, *emotions* usually aren't. If you spill a cup of coffee in a restaurant, the initial feeling will produce a slight adrenaline rush and a minor physical tension as you jump back to avoid being burned by the hot liquid. However, if you then move to the emotion of self-consciousness or embarrassment about the spill, blood rushes to your face, you blush from head to toe, and you may even reactively cringe. Or when someone criticizes you, you might sense the feeling of wariness as a brief frown that passes over your

A Johns Hopkins study, funded by the National Institute of Health (NIH) and the Lucille P. Markey Foundation Charitable Trust, of Palo Alto, California, tracked 1,055 medical students for a period of thirty-six years during medical school and the years following. The study found that "men—who said they expressed or concealed their anger, became irritable or engaged in gripe sessions—were five times more likely than their calmer counterparts to have an early heart attack even without a family history of heart disease." Additionally, "hot tempers predicted disease long before other traditional risk factors like diabetes and hypertension became apparent," says Patricia P. Chang, M.D., lead author of the study and a cardiology fellow. (Patricia P. Chang et al., "Anger in Young Men and Subsequent Premature Cardiovascular Disease: The Precursors Study," *Archives of Internal Medicine*, 162, April 22, 2002: 901-906)

forehead. But if that feeling moves to the emotion of rage, your ears will burn, your face will become red and hot, your jaw (and fists!) might clench, and your heart will pound.

Strong emotion also tends to get stuck in the body whereas physiological responses based on feeling are more fleeting and last only as long as necessary for the situation. In the example of being cut off in traffic, the physiological response caused by the feeling—adrenaline rush, quick tensing of the muscles to help you swerve out of harm's way—takes just a few moments to dissipate. But the response caused by the story-produced emotion—tense muscles, fast heart rate, shallow ragged breathing—remains in the body for much longer, and reinstates itself whenever you review the incident with yourself or others.

From Feeling to Emotion

As I mentioned, the movement from feeling to emotion can be quick and hard to recognize. Let's use some everyday examples: What do you feel when someone compliments you about your work or your appearance? For

> ### EXERCISE: **Releasing Emotion from the Body**
>
> In later chapters, we will discuss the role of breathing more fully. But this simple exercise will help you release strong emotion and its toxic effects from the body.
>
> First, acknowledge the emotion. Admit that it is present and name it. Next, allow yourself to feel it fully. Where is it located in your body? How does it feel? Finally, breathe deeply and slowly. As you inhale, acknowledge the emotion. As you exhale, imagine that you are releasing it and its toxins. Inhale and exhale at least ten times or until you feel the emotion dissipate.

most of us, the initial experience is a pleasant feeling of being appreciated. But depending on your conditioning, that feeling may quickly morph into the emotion of self-consciousness or unworthiness with the accompanying story that you are never good enough. On the other hand, if your underlying story claims that you are deserving and worthy, the feeling may expand into the emotion of pride or self-satisfaction. Same initial feeling, two different emotions based on two different stories or conditioned beliefs.

> The greatest griefs are those we cause ourselves.
>
> —*Sophocles*

Take another example: being out in public and spilling your drink all over yourself. Pretty common occurrence (at least it is in my life!). Perhaps you stumble or someone bumps you, and you realize that you are about to wear your drink all over your shirt. The initial feeling is that quick sense of "oops!" as you recognize that something is about to happen that you don't want, accompanied by your body's physical reaction as it shifts to balance itself and avoid the spill. That feeling will be common to almost all of us.

But what happens next, the emotion that follows is individual. If you have an underlying belief that you are a klutz and that people will ridicule you for clumsiness, your emotion might be humiliation, embarrassment, or shame (or all three!). But if your conditioned story says that people and circumstances are always out to get you and make you look bad, your emotion might be one of anger. You might feel victimized and search for someone or something to blame. The feeling responded appropriately to the situation. The emotion sprang from an underlying belief or story.

Emotion Leaves No Choice

Whereas a feeling may inform your conscious choices, emotion usurps your ability to choose. Because emotion stems from your conditioning, it triggers you into reactive mode, insisting that you replay old patterns of

EXERCISE: **Your Place of Choice**

I have asked you to explore your own stories and even to make up different stories than your conditioned ones. Now I'm going to ask you to try telling no story at all! This takes a little practice, but can help you tune into your *moment of choice* before a conditioned story and emotion take hold.

As you go through your day, notice the incidents that trigger an emotion. For instance, what if your spouse comes home very late from work without calling? In that moment, stop, take a deep breath, and say to yourself, "My spouse is late. Period." Do not allow your conditioned story to tell itself! Do not start ranting about how inconsiderate he or she is or, "If my spouse really loved me, he would have called." No! "My spouse is late. Period." Make sure that "Period" is firm.

Another example: You go out for lunch and there is a long delay before you are served. What do you say to yourself? "My food has been delayed. Period."

Play this game in as many situations as you can. You will begin to notice that without a story and its emotion to push you around, you are free to make choices about your response to the situation. And without the chatter in your head and the emotions roiling through your body, you just might find that your thinking is clearer, more solution-oriented, and more creative.

behavior. Like all conditioning, it feels automatic and almost out of your control.

Imagine watching your child playing in a park. You are relaxed and enjoying the moment. Suddenly you notice your child attempting a tricky maneuver on the jungle gym. Your initial feeling might be of heightened awareness and a sense of preparedness for action, should it become necessary. But if your brain has been conditioned to believe that it is dangerous for children to take risks, the emotion of fear might cause you to become overly protective, leap up to disrupt your child's exploration, and scold him or her for even trying something new.

Or imagine being criticized by a coworker during an important meeting at work. Your initial feeling may be a slight sense of wariness and heightened attention to the criticizer and the situation. But if you have a deepseated story that any criticism is a personal attack and a threat to your survival, your fury might push you to respond aggressively and angrily. The feeling would have allowed you to choose how to respond to the criticism: You could learn from the criticism or dispute it; you could apologize for the action that was criticized or explain it more fully. Whatever you chose to do next, it would be a conscious choice. But once you are operating with strong emotion, you are almost forced to react in ways that may or may not be appropriate.

Emotions Are Not So Bright

Emotions are certainly not inherently bad or evil, but they don't have the instinctual intelligence of feelings. Emotions are tied up with the conditioned beliefs or stories that have been hardwired into our brains, and they cause us to be reactive rather than making conscious choices about our actions. Some of these unconscious reactions turn out to be good or benign, but others do not serve us or our goals at all.

For instance, a friend of mine blew his knee out skiing when he tried to out-ski his daughter's new boyfriend, a man thirty years younger. Can you guess the emotion and "knee-jerk" conditioned re-action behind that one? I once fired my landscaper in a self-righteous huff. Two hours later, a truckload of trees arrived for my yard—but of course, I had no one to plant them! Haven't we all gotten swept up in an emotional moment only to say or do something we wish we could take back?

> If you are patient in one moment of anger, you will escape a hundred days of sorrow.
>
> —*Chinese proverb*

Carving a Vicious Cycle

Emotions can be overwhelming, so we look for ways to manage them. Some of our coping techniques are not that positive, yet they still get carved into our brains. For instance, many of us try to funnel emotion into nonproductive action: You're hurt by something your boss said, so you reach for your stash of cookies. Your wife's nagging makes you feel demeaned, so you go out drinking. You're angered about the political cli-mate, so you pick a fight about it with your neighbor. You're panicked about your finances, so you yell at your kid.

Though cookies, drinking, fighting, or yelling don't really address the negative emotion, the brain begins to associate the action with the emo-tion. Eating cookies feels good and temporarily distracts from the pain of hurt, and more cookies may distract even more. After a few feeling-hurt-so-hit-the-cookies cycles, a neuropathway is carved into the brain that connects emotional pain with cookies. At a certain point the urge to eat cookies whenever you are sad becomes powerful, and despite your conscious knowledge that it is not healthy, fighting the urge seems im-possible.

We don't just funnel *negative* emotions into nonproductive action. We often respond to strong *positive* emotion inappropriately. You fall in love

Researchers at the University of Ontario recruited a group of 394 women, ages 18–25, from a large urban center to investigate the development of eating disorders in young women. The women completed research questionnaires assessing the level at which they engaged in self-silencing of needs and voice, the suppression of the outward expression of anger, and the internalization of the objectified gaze toward one's own body. The results of this study showed that "a greater tendency in women to silence their own needs in light of others' expectations, to suppress the outward expression of anger, and to objectify one's own body *predicts* disordered eating patterns and body weight." (Niva Piran and Holly C. Cormier, "The Social Construction of Women and Disordered Eating Patterns," *Journal of Counseling Psychology*, 52, no. 4, October 2005: 549–558.)

with someone, so you accommodate his or her every need at the expense of your own needs and desires. You feel so proud of your accomplishments at work that you become a workaholic. You adore your grandchildren, so you buy them everything they ask for.

After a few repetitions, these unhealthy coping tools become conditioned reactive responses, especially if accompanied by strong emotion. They are meant to dull the pain of negative emotions or enhance the enjoyment of positive ones, but they rarely hit the mark. However, because these poor coping patterns become hardwired into our brains, we default to them whenever the emotion associated with the pattern pops up.

Feelings: Innocent and Wise

Feelings, unlike emotions, are extremely intelligent. Not only do they support whatever we focus on, but they respond appropriately to the environment. When feeling has not been wrapped around a story or belief to become emotion, it offers an uncanny wisdom and is worth paying attention to. Feelings are terrific receptors and can pick up information that we don't consciously pick up. They represent our instinctual or intuitive inner wisdom.

EXERCISE: **Taking Inventory**

Spend a few moments to take inventory of coping mechanisms you have used that do not really serve you. What triggers them? How do they initially seem to offer relief from a negative emotion or add pleasure to a positive one? What about them does not serve you?

As you do this, keep the perspective that these coping behaviors have been hardwired into your brain. There is no need (and no point) for you to feel bad or guilty about these patterns. The object is to bring them to awareness and make a choice. If these behaviors are not what you want, acknowledging their existence is the first step to rewiring your brain with something you *do* want!

Most of us have experienced this wisdom. For example, have you ever been in a bad relationship and after it was all over, said "You know, before we started, I had a little feeling that it just wouldn't work out." Or maybe you've looked at your child and just *knew* that something was wrong. Or you've been offered a career or investment opportunity and your gut instinct told you not to pursue it.

Have you ever noticed that this gut instinct or feeling has no story to go with it? You know there's something wrong with your child but you don't know *how* you know. You sensed red flags about a relationship or decision but couldn't quite explain what they were. You feel the clear message to act or not act but you are not sure why, so you make up a rationale for your action afterward!

We've all experienced the wisdom of feelings. But because they can be very subtle, a quick blip that bubbles to the surface then disappears, they are easy to miss if you're not paying attention. And, because most of us are more familiar with the emotion that often follows the feeling than the feeling itself, we might miss the feeling and its message entirely.

Additionally, many of us, especially in modern Western cultures, have been conditioned to ignore, deny, or suppress feelings. With no storylines

---

EXERCISE: You've Already Been There

Almost all of us have stumbled into the wisdom of our feelings. You might have called it gut instinct. You might know it as intuition. Whatever name you call it, remember those times that you were aware of, and perhaps acted from, that feeling sense. What was the context? How did you experience it? Did it feel natural? Scary? Exciting? Weird? Would you recognize that feeling sense again?

---

or conditioned beliefs attached to them, feelings have seemed less rational and illogical, perhaps less reliable, than analytical thinking. But feelings are being recognized once again for their validity and the value they bring to our life experience. More and more of us are tuning into our feeling sense, training ourselves to listen to this "still, small voice."

Emotion and Feelings as Tools

So with regard to emotions and feelings, our mission is to:

- Distinguish between our own feelings and emotions on an experiential level
- Learn to work *with* the emotion that arises from our conditioning in positive ways
- Instill emotion into the new conscious conditioning we wish to hardwire into our brains
- Become more attuned to our feelings to be able to harness their tremendous power and wisdom.

By now, you are probably coming to a good understanding of distinguishing between feeling and emotion. In future chapters, we will delve further into conscious conditioning and becoming more attuned to our

In 2005, Harvard Medical School researchers studied the relationship between positive feelings, specifically hope and curiosity, and health. Their particular interest was whether people with higher levels of these positive feelings might be less likely to develop hypertension, diabetes, or respiratory tract infections. They examined the medical records of 1,041 patients over a two-year period and assessed their level of positive feelings using a mail-in questionnaire. The results showed that higher levels of hope were associated with a decreased likelihood of having or developing a disease. Higher levels of curiosity were also associated with decreased likelihood of hypertension and diabetes mellitus. The research suggests that positive emotion may play a protective role in the development of disease. (L. S. Richman, L. Kubzansky, J. Maselko, I. Kawachi, P. Choo, and M. Bauer, "Positive Emotion and Health: Going Beyond the Negative," *Health Psychology*, 24, no. 4, 2005: 422–429.)

feelings. And, because emotions hold so much power over our lives, I'd like to expand on the steps that will help you work with emotions effectively, even while their conditioned stories or beliefs remain in place.

Your first step is to *acknowledge* what you are experiencing right in the moment. Whether you are pleased with your emotional response or not, it never works in the long run to deny it. Denying an emotion or trying to submerge it typically gives it more strength. For instance, if you don't allow yourself to experience your irritability, it often simmers and eventually explodes as anger. So acknowledge whatever the emotion is, name it, and allow yourself to feel it.

The creative is the place where no one else has ever been. You have to leave the city of your comfort and go into the wilderness of your intuition. What you'll discover will be wonderful. What you'll discover will be yourself.

—*Alan Alda*

Step two is to *identify* how the emotion typically causes you to react. Does your irritability push you into an argument with your partner? Do you swallow your irritation and clam up? Do you browbeat yourself for feeling irritable? What reaction is triggered?

This is often where the underlying conditioned story or belief that is attached to the emotion announces itself. "Good people take things in stride." "If I don't defend myself, people will walk all over me." Keep in mind that your conditioned belief will usually sound absolutely true! Whatever the story is, simply take note of it.

The third step is to *breathe*. Take long, slow, deep breaths. Breathing clears the mind and releases tension and anxiety from the body. Your awareness is brought back to the moment. Your breath helps you unplug the emotion from your body and allows you to take back the power from your automatic emotional reaction. It puts you in the place of choice again.

Next, *activate a more positive feeling or emotion*. You may not be able to leap to joy and excitement from your feeling of irritability. But you can probably experience a sense of calm or ease, maybe centeredness or openness. If you can't automatically ease into a better pure feeling, give yourself a story that will initiate an emotion, such as, "I am safe and my life is good. I have everything I need." By consciously shifting from an unwanted negative emotion to a neutral or positive feeling or emotion, we loosen the unwanted emotion's hold and break up the cycle of its automatic reaction in that moment. This is how we move forward, one moment at a time. By taking life in small, bite-size pieces, we become capable and competent of handling whatever comes our way.

> It is only by following your deepest instinct that you can lead a rich life, and if you let your fear of consequence prevent you from following your deepest instinct, then your life will be safe, expedient and thin.
>
> —*Katherine Butler Hathaway*

Finally, ask yourself, "What is the most important thing for me right now?" In your consciously chosen state of calm and centeredness, you reconnect with the intelligence of your feelings, think more clearly, and will find that the answer will come. It will undoubtedly be clearer and more life-affirming than your reaction in the throes of emotion could be! Act on this answer, and as you act on what is most important and aligned for you in that moment, you are retraining your brain and nervous system to respond from a calmer and more centered place.

Chapter 5

Power of Breath

Two monks, master and student, walked along a path, returning to their monastery after several hours of meditating high in the Himalayan Mountains. The student complained to his master, saying, "Breathing is so boring!" Without a word, the master grabbed his student by the neck, pulled him over to a nearby stream, and plunged the student's head beneath the rushing water. He kept him underwater for several seconds, as the student kicked and squirmed. Finally, the master yanked his student's head above the surface and asked, "Now, what do you have to say about breathing?"

Obviously, as the master reminded his student, breathing is critical to life itself. But *proper* breathing also has a critical impact on physical health, emotional well-being, mental clarity, and even spiritual connection. It is crucial to keeping the brain healthy and fit, and it is essential to the process of rewiring your brain. Spiritual practices have recognized the power of breath for centuries. Today, medical science is starting to explore its physical and psychological benefits.

> Listen, are you breath-
> ing just a little, and call-
> ing it a life?
>
> —*Mary Oliver*

There is a substantial difference between the way most of us breathe on a daily basis and proper *belly* breathing. But before we discuss those differences, let's look at how breath affects our systems.

Breath Basics

As you inhale, the breath enters the body and goes into the lungs. Air enters through the middle lobe, and as more air enters, the upper and lower lobes of the lungs are filled. Within the lungs, blood takes the oxygen from the breath, exchanging it for toxins and waste products that are then released with the exhale. The oxygen travels in the blood throughout the body, purifying the blood and thus delivering energy to all organs and cells.

Breath and Physical Health

The shallow breathing most of us use can lead to a constriction of the chest and lung tissue over time, decreasing oxygen flow and delivery to all our major organs. When we consistently breathe with our chest, and not deeply into our bellies, our bodies maintain irregularly high levels of carbon dioxide in our blood. What does this mean? It means that we are not inhaling enough oxygen or exhaling enough carbon dioxide. This leads to problems such as fatigue, mental fog, and decreased organ and tissue function.

Michael G. White, health educator and author writes, "The average person reaches peak respiratory function and lung capacity in their mid 20's. Then they begin to lose respiratory capacity: between 10 and 27 percent for every decade of life! So, unless you are doing something to maintain or improve your breathing capacity, it will decline, and with it, your general health, your life expectancy, and for that matter, your spirit too!" (www .breathing.com)

Think about that statistic: if we lose 10 percent to 27 percent of our lung capacity every year, we are losing 10 percent to 27 percent of our ability to exhale toxins as well. Our breathing is responsible for releasing 70 percent of all toxins and waste entering and produced by the body; elimination and sweating release the remaining 30 percent. The volume of waste and toxins entering and created by our bodies certainly doesn't decrease as we age. So if our lungs lose capacity over the years and their ability to release toxins is compromised, where do all those unreleased toxins go? Research shows that these unreleased toxins sit in our cells. As scary as this sounds, the good news is that we can reverse this process by learning how to breathe properly.

Researchers have found some interesting results when they teach patients to use belly breathing. Regular, deep breathing has been found to help manage hypertension, diabetes, eating disorders, and even obesity. Studies show that deep slow breathing for ten to twenty minutes per day on a regular basis significantly lowers blood pressure to the extent that patients are able to discontinue using their blood pressure medication—*and* that these benefits are lost if the patient suspends their breathing practice.

Connections between physical health and proper breathing are still being made in the world of medicine. It is interesting to note, however, that

In a 2001 study of thirty-three individuals with essential hypertension, researchers found that daily brief sessions of slow and regular breathing lowered blood pressure. Over a period of eight weeks, these patients used a device, Breathe with Interactive Music (BIM), to guide them in slow and regular breathing for ten minutes each day. At the end of the eight-week period, results showed significantly lowered blood pressure. (E. Grossman, A. Grossman, M. H. Schein, R. Zimlichman, and B. Gavish, "Breathing-Control Lowers Blood Pressure," *Journal of Human Hypertension*, 15, no. 4, April 2001: 263–269.)

belly breathing is now being used, endorsed, or taught by leading institutions such as the Harvard Medical School, the Mayo Clinic, Johns Hopkins, Rush Presbyterian Hospital, and the American Heart Association.

All of this science only verifies what our bodies instinctively know. But in modern times, we have been hardwired to ignore what our bodies are telling us. We listen more carefully to the functioning of our cars more than we do to the functioning of our bodies! We have come to interpret pain or discomfort as something to eliminate by medication, rather than a valuable signal that our physical system is out of balance. We have ignored our bodies' inherent healing systems in deference to external interventions. That trend is now changing in Western medicine. Health professionals are now often looking at approaches that integrate our bodies' capabilities for self-healing and medical treatment.

Breath and Emotional Health

How does deep breathing affect our emotions and ability to think clearly? In times of stress, our body goes to its survival response, the fight or flight mechanism, and it releases large amounts of cortisol and adrenaline. This

In the Johns Hopkins study investigating anger and cardiovascular disease (cited previously), lead author Patricia P. Chang, M.D., speaks to the deleterious effects of anger, saying that when we're in the throes of anger "evidence points to stress-related release of extra catecholamines. These substances, such as adrenaline, prepare the body to meet emergencies (whether real or not), by constricting blood vessels and forcing the heart to work harder to supply the body with fresh blood. In other words, the experience of anger activates our system to work overtime, regardless of whether the threat is real or not." (Patricia P. Chang et al., "Anger in Young Men and Subsequent Premature Cardiovascular Disease: The Precursors Study," *Archives of Internal Medicine*, April 22, 2002; 2002; 162: 901–906).

mechanism was hardwired into our brains centuries ago as an intelligent response to dangerous
and threatening life situations and is controlled by
the sympathetic nervous system.

> Breathe. Let go. And re-
> mind yourself that this
> very moment is the only
> one you know you have
> for sure.
>
> —*Oprah Winfrey*

However, modern life carries with it a level of
stress that calls up this survival response whether it
is warranted or not. Urgent deadlines, competing
priorities, lives that require too many spinning plates at once—all of this
keeps our sympathetic nervous systems on alert. Unfortunately, when the
survival response persists over extended periods of time, the chemicals it
releases can cause great harm to our bodies.

Deep belly breathing is the most effective and efficient way to turn
off the survival response. In fact, it is the only mechanism we can consciously use to do so! Our deep breathing signals our brain that all is well.
The brain then activates our parasympathetic nervous system, the coun-
terpart to the sympathetic nervous system, to produce the relaxation response. It slows down and calms our system (which the adrenaline of the
survival response has thrown into chaos). Beyond stress, research shows
that regular deep breathing can be helpful in handling clinical depression, anxiety, and other stress-related diseases.

In a study published by the Mind/Body Medical Institute at Harvard Medical School, researchers investigated whether there was a therapeutic
connection between the relaxation response and stress-related diseases.
They found the relaxation response to be an "appropriate and relevant
therapeutic tool to counteract several stress-related disease processes and
certain health-restrictions." (Tobias Esch, Gregory Fricchione, and George
Stefano, "The Therapeutic Use of the Relaxation Response in Stress-Related Diseases," *Medical Science Monitor*, no. 2, 2003: RA23–34.)

It's interesting to have the scientific explanation and validation, but isn't this common sense? What did your mother tell you when you were angry or upset? "Take a deep breath and count to ten." When you were smart enough to follow Mom's advice, didn't you notice how much better you felt? That your mind cleared, your emotions calmed, your heart stopped pounding?

Breathing's direct connection to our emotional states and moods is pretty obvious when you stop to notice it. When you're angry, afraid, or upset, your breathing is naturally rapid, shallow, and ragged. But it's hard to remain upset if you consciously breathe slowly and deeply with a regulated rhythm. You can't always talk yourself into feeling calm and centered, but when you consciously breathe deeply, your parasympathetic system kicks in to produce the calm you desire.

And here's a breathing bonus: Studies show that five minutes of deep breathing, accompanied by a feeling of appreciation or gratitude, releases enough endorphins to counteract the toxins created by anger or stress. So not only can deep breathing stop harmful chemicals from being released into your body, it can trigger beneficial ones to help repair the damage!

EXERCISE: **Prove It to Yourself**

Think about a situation that normally upsets or angers you. Allow yourself to get fully into the negative emotion you typically feel and the thoughts you normally have in this situation. How would you describe your physical and emotional state? And, without changing anything, notice your breathing. How would you characterize it?

Next, consciously slow your breathing down and deepen it. Take at least ten deep, slow breaths. What changes do you sense in your body? How have your emotions shifted? What about your thinking?

Even though it's tough to admit, you probably found that Mom was right about this one!

Breathing and Mental Clarity

Your brain has around a hundred billion brain cells and each of these cells uses oxygen to function. In fact, your brain's need for oxygen is more than ten times greater than the rest of your body! The brain is our body's most energetic organ, consuming at least 20 percent of the body's calories even at rest. But unlike other organs or muscle cells, the brain cannot store energy and needs a constant supply of glucose and oxygen in its blood supply. Active brain cells (neurons) need a better blood supply than idle cells, a supply that is especially rich in oxygen and nutrients. This healthy supply of oxygen and a variety of nutrients enhances the cells' function. Neurons are particularly vulnerable to inadequate oxygen supply. Healthy respiratory functioning increases oxygen in the brain, improves neuronal glucose metabolism, enhances general neuronal metabolism, supports antioxidant defenses, and generally increases efficiency and functioning of the brain.

Brain power can be increased when people take extra supplies of either of the two basic neural fuels, glucose and oxygen. In one study, volunteers who were given a blast of oxygen remembered 20 percent more of the words on a list, had improved concentration for up to six hours, improved their performance on computer games, and scored better on arithmetic tests. On the flip side, other studies show that a primary cause of brain degeneration is the decline of respiratory functioning.

So how does this apply to us on a practical level? First of all, if our brains require so much of our oxygen supply to function and we're letting our lungs lose 9 percent to 25 percent of their capacity every year, we're obviously in for trouble! Also, many of us now work in sedentary positions. We're focused on our computers all day, barely moving. This lack of activity usually means that our breathing remains shallow. And many of us habitually "hold our breath" when we concentrate or are feeling stressed, a habit that cuts off our natural source of clarity and focus.

There's Breathing . . . and There's Breathing

Everyone knows how to breathe, right? Well, yes and no. Actually, there is really nothing new about belly breathing, every infant on the planet has mastered it. We come into this world breathing naturally and using our body's organs most effectively. Breathing is a *natural skill* that, for most of us, has become lost, forgotten, or simply taken for granted. As infants and children, we breathed easily and deeply into all three lobes of our lungs without thinking about it.

> Most men pursue pleasure with such breathless haste that they hurry past it.
>
> —*Soren Kierkegaard*

But as adults, most of us moved to a shallow chest breathing pattern during the day and that shallow chest breathing only partially fills our lungs. We only revert to the fuller belly breathing of our childhood as we relax before falling into sleep. Why is this? There are various theories, such as tension held in the body, the relative newness of the upright position for our species, cultural norms of holding our tummies in, stress in our days, and overactive mental activity. But whatever the cause, most of us breathe in ways that do not fully

EXERCISE: **Are You a Belly Breather or a Chest Breather?**

Let's find out. Without consciously changing the way you are breathing right now, place one hand on your chest and one hand over your belly button. Keep breathing the way you usually breathe. Notice your rhythm without changing it. Notice which hand—the one on your belly or the one on your chest—moves more as you breathe.

If you are belly breathing, the hand on your belly will rise as you inhale and fall as you exhale. On the inhale, your diaphragm descends, creating more space within your lungs for air to enter which makes your belly rise. As you exhale, your lungs empty, your diaphragm ascends, and your belly lowers. If you are chest breathing, you may find the opposite to be true: Your belly may constrict when you inhale and expand when you inhale!

Try this experiment again when you lie down to rest or go to sleep. Without consciously changing your breathing pattern, you may find that you slip naturally into a belly breathing mode.

nourish our bodies or produce the positive effects deep belly breathing can offer us.

Healthy belly breathing has a slow, steady rhythm. The muscles of belly and chest remain relaxed as air moves deeply into and out of the lungs. It is marked by the rhythmic movement of the belly rather than a rising and falling of the chest. The antithesis of this type of healthy breathing is the tight shallow breathing of stress or anger.

Because so many of us have developed poor breathing habits and because it is so essential, I've spent many hours in workshops and one-on-one sessions teaching people how to breathe, helping them find their personal rhythm. This step, learning to breathe properly, is crucial for the processes that rewire the brain.

If you just discovered that you are a chest breather, don't despair! Ninety-nine percent of my clients are initially chest breathers. Retraining

> I am open to receive with every breath I breathe.
>
> —*Michael Sun*

your breathing pattern may at first seem awkward, but it is not difficult. And once you get the hang of it, it's easy to notice when you have reverted to chest breathing and to switch to your new healthy breathing mode.

So let's learn how to breathe the way our body organically prefers to breathe.

Please note that all of these exercises are on the CD that accompanies this book.

EXERCISE: Baby Breath

First, stand with your knees slightly bent and relaxed, and tilt your tailbone slightly forward. If standing is uncomfortable or difficult, then lie down. Relax your jaw, let your tongue float to help you get into a relaxed state. Relax the muscles of your belly.

Lightly place a hand over your belly button. Inhale and imagine your breath filling the middle lobe of your lungs then spreading to the lower and upper lobes. Rather than forcing the breath, think of your belly as a bellows, naturally drawing in air as it expands and expelling air as it collapses.

Next, inhale to a slow count of four. Feel air filling your lungs and feel the hand on your belly rise. Exhale slowly, to a count of six. Feel the hand on your belly lower as the air leaves your body. Pause briefly at the end of your exhale. It is on the exhale that your body activates the parasympathetic nervous system, the relaxation response.

Note: Do not tighten your belly in order to make your exhale last longer. Keep it relaxed and let it collapse naturally.

Continue the pattern of four-count inhale, six-count exhale, and pause. Imagine that your breath fills all three lobes of your lungs. This imagery will help retrain your body so that belly breathing becomes your natural breathing pattern again.

How does that feel? Do you feel relaxed? Energized? Anxious? Pay attention to what you are experiencing during and after the exercise. Dizziness, confusion, or anxiety means you should stop the exercise and take a short break. You can try again in a minute or two after the feeling has subsided. If you felt anxious, the pace of your breathing might have been too fast or you might have been using your chest and not breathing with your belly.

Optimal times to begin your practice and develop your breathing skill are when you first wake up in the morning and just as you lay your head on your pillow at night. But you can also practice while sitting in traffic, standing in the grocery line, or watching TV—especially during commercials!

Under Stress

Most of us do not breathe properly, but this is especially true when we are under stress, angry, or upset. So, once you feel comfortable with your breathing skill, practice belly breathing in situations of increasing unease. You will be amazed at the power of your breathing, particularly the first time you realize that intense emotions (those emotions that used to trigger unwanted reactions) can be calmed, and you can return to a balanced and focused state just by activating a few deep, slow belly breaths. When you exhale deeply, your body releases the negative energy caused by the experience of being overwhelmed, stressed, frustrated, and angry. We can take

---

EXERCISE: Stress Test

Earlier, I asked you to take some deep breaths while thinking about a stressful situation. Repeat that exercise, thinking of a typically upsetting situation. Only this time, use the breathing pattern of a four-count inhale, six-count exhale, and pause. You will probably notice even more benefit!

Now, let's up the ante and take this skill into real life. Next time you find yourself in a truly stressful situation that is moving into anger or upset, pause and do at least a few good belly breaths—twenty cycles is optimal. If you forget to breathe in that difficult moment, do a few deep belly breaths as soon as you remember.

Note: In public, you don't necessarily have to place your hand on your belly button!

charge of our emotions again simply by learning how to breathe properly. Really, it is that easy!

"But in the middle of a fight, emergency, or panic, how can I take the time to stop and breathe?!" How can you *not*? The few moments it takes to do your deep breathing will give you the power, clarity, and calm you need to deal with the situation effectively. *And*, it will cleanse the toxic chemicals of stress from your system.

My client Susan, a seventy-four-year-old widow, came to me saying, "I don't want to be known as an angry old woman!" She talked about constant arguments with her children, their spouses, and her grandchildren. "I don't think it's my fault. I don't feel angry, and I don't know why I seem to be causing trouble, but I must be."

It took several sessions before Susan could admit to her angry feelings. "I was never allowed to be angry, so I don't know what it feels like or if I would know how to recognize it." I asked her to observe her daily interactions more carefully and taught her to belly breathe. We practiced over several sessions using role play to elicit negative emotions so she would be prepared when those feelings arose in daily life.

Susan's *ah-ha!* experience came when she was watching a TV news program with her grandson. Susan voiced her opinion about a particular story, to which her grandson said: "Oh that's so stupid, Grandma!" In the moment just following her grandson's remark, Susan sat still as she allowed her anger to well up inside.

"I thought either I was having a heart attack or I was experiencing real anger for the first time in my life. I did what you've suggested and focused my attention on my breathing. Well, in a couple of seconds, which seemed like forever, I didn't feel angry anymore. I actually felt fine."

Then something surprising happened. After a few moments of silence, Susan's grandson turned to her and said, "I'm sorry Grandma. That was rude of me." In the past, Susan would have exploded, her grandson would have retorted, and the argument would have raged for weeks. By using her deep breathing, Susan allowed the situation to resolve itself perfectly.

Within that incident and her moments of breathing, Susan realized that (a) she could recognize her emotions, (b) it was okay to have them, and (c) that these emotions no longer had the power to control her actions or thinking.

Part of Your Daily Routine

As you move through your day, pause and notice your breathing. Initially, you may need to leave notes for yourself to remember to do this! Especially notice when you are not breathing properly, in what type of circumstance and in whose company. Many people hold their breath while concentrating on something important or difficult, when they are nervous, angry, or frightened. Improper breathing at these critical times minimizes your clarity and ability to consciously choose your response to the situation. Inadequate breathing often leads you to, and keeps you stuck in, your default conditioned reactions, the ones that have been hardwired into your brain, and these conditioned reactions to events may not be your best choice. When you notice that a situation has triggered shallower breathing, consciously move to the deeper belly breathing you've practiced: four-count inhale, six-count exhale, pause. Try practicing your breathing while you brush your teeth, while you eat a meal, while working or gardening, or just before going to sleep (which will set you up to practice through the night!)

By consciously switching to better breathing within both comfortable and difficult situations, you are actually rewiring your brain and rebalancing your nervous system. This will allow you to respond to life's tasks and stressors with more patience, ease, comfort, effectiveness, and, most importantly, with conscious choice.

EXERCISE: **Breathe in Health**

Settle into a comfortable position and begin with your deep, slow belly breathing at a pace of six to nine breaths per minute. As you get into your rhythm, imagine each organ receiving maximal amounts of oxygen. Focus your attention on your breath as it moves in and out of your body. Imagine that your entire body is breathing, each organ, each muscle, each cell. Next place particular attention on those organs that are in distress. Sense or visualize these organs inhaling oxygen and health, then exhaling toxins and waste.

To get optimal benefit, I recommend that my clients do this exercise for ten- to twenty-minute sessions twice per day. But doing it whenever you think of it is certainly better than not doing it at all!

Breathing for Health

There are many diseases for which you can reap the benefits of deep breathing. Slow deep belly breathing is the only fully natural treatment for hypertension (high blood pressure) that is recognized by the medical profession. For clients dealing with these and other health challenges, I recommend the following exercise to help bring all of the body's systems into balance.

Another common complaint that breathing can relieve is insomnia. Did you know that 74 percent of Americans suffer from sleeplessness? If you are one of them, or even for the occasional bout of tossing and turning, try the following exercise just after shutting off the lights and lying down in bed.

As you move into sleep, this wonderful feeling will be the last feeling of the day. Breathing with good feelings does remarkable things for your body. Not only will it help to relieve your sleeplessness, but the vitality hormone (DHEA) will flow in your system throughout the night nourishing every cell of your body. If you practice this every night for five to fifteen

EXERCISE: Breathe Yourself to Sleep

As your head relaxes on your pillow, begin your deep belly breathing and find your rhythm. Focus on your breathing to allow your mind to clear of any chatter or concerns of the day.

As you continue breathing, recall of something pleasant from your day—or if that particular day had few pleasant experiences, pick something pleasant from another time. Bring up just enough detail about those pleasant moments to re-experience the pleasurable feelings they brought you. Continue for a few minutes, breathing that good feeling into your body.

minutes, you'll soon find yourself sleeping through the night. Activating and breathing with positive feelings can be that powerful.

Breathing to Rewire Your Brain

Proper breathing will be critical to the process of rewiring the limited beliefs and negative conditioning that are holding you back. Breathing fully and deeply calms the nervous system and increases blood flow to the brain. This allows us to (1) be aware of thought patterns that are not working in our best interest, (2) acknowledge these patterns, (3) release them, and (4) plug in new, more empowering, and life-affirming thoughts. In later chapters, we will run through specific exercises designed to modify the hardwiring of our brains to support what we desire. Deep breathing will be key to all of these exercises.

The beauty of breathing is that it is available to all of us! It's absolutely free and we already possess the equipment to do it. We don't have to attend classes or engage expensive breathing coaches for it. We just need to become more aware of it and appreciate what it can do for us. Once you learn proper breathing, you can use it to enhance your experience of being

> Breathe in the elixir of life,
> Cast off your doubt.
> In every breath there's strife.
> Let it in; let it out.
>
> —*Ronald W. Hull*

alive: to accomplish goals, enhance health, feel less anxiety, experience more focus and control over automatic reactions, and achieve the happiness you desire. Practice the breathing exercises on the CDs to experience the rhythm and deepen your breathing practice.

So take a deep breath, and read on.

Chapter 6

Power of Imagination

In past chapters, you have seen how your brain (and with it, your entire physiology) responds to the beliefs and stories it has been given. If your conditioned belief says that you are a klutz, your body proves it by tripping over anything in its path. If your underlying story claims that all salesmen are crooks, your brain will direct you to every unethical salesperson in town. Many of these stories are false, but your brain doesn't distinguish between what is false or true. It dutifully responds to each story, how strongly you feel about it, and how often you tell it. It recruits your entire physiology to make sure your stories and beliefs become real.

Earl Nightingale used to compare the brain to a plot of farmland. He said that the brain does not care what you plant in it, deadly nightshade or wonderful fruit. The brain will support either, just like the land. Many of the stories that rule our lives and shape our reality have been carved into our brains unconsciously. And as you are beginning to see, many of these stories do not serve us. Fortunately, you have the ability to plant different stories in your powerful brain, using a tool that you possess naturally: your imagination.

It's All in Your Head?

Studies show that our brains and physiology will respond not only to an event or situation that is actually happening, but also to those we entertain mentally. In other words, when we think about something deeply enough, our brains and bodies react as if that thing was really occurring. Though you may not have sophisticated neuroscientific equipment to prove this to yourself, you have encountered it in your own experience.

> Imagination is everything. It is the preview of life's coming attractions.
>
> —*Albert Einstein*

Take a moment to think about a sad event from your past. Let yourself remember it in detail: What was happening, who was there, where did it happen? What did this mean to you at the time? As you think of this event, notice how you feel. Unless you have stuffed your feelings in some hidden corner of your psyche, you are probably experiencing emotions that are similar to what you felt then: sadness, grief, hurt. You probably feel that same ache in the chest, hole in the pit of the stomach, urge to cry. (If you don't feel anything or very little with the memory of a sad event, it's likely that your feelings have been suppressed. When we don't allow ourselves to experience a strong feeling, we may be numb to it but that feeling becomes locked within our physiology. If this might be the case for you, turn to Chapter 7 for a process to help you get back in touch with your feelings.) Clearly, the sad event is not happening in this moment, but your brain and body are responding as if it is. Your brain and physiology are responding to a *mental* image.

> Imagination: Being able to think of things that haven't appeared on TV yet.
>
> —*Henry Beard*

Take another example: watching an action thriller where a heroine is chased by a serial killer through a darkened house. Don't you feel your entire system responding? Your pulse races, you feel nervous, your body is tense—all based on a fictitious situation with a fictitious character. How many of us could read *The Yearling* or *The Diary of Anne Frank* without shedding a few tears? We even feel excited and happy during Saturday

Alvaro Pascual-Leone, chief of the Beth Israel Deaconess Medical Center, Harvard Medical School, has conducted experiments that show we can change the structure of our brains simply by using our imagination. In 1995, Pascual-Leone took subjects who had never studied piano, taught them a one-handed, five-finger exercise on the piano and then let them hear the notes as they played. These subjects were then randomly assigned to a physical practice group or a mental practice (visualization) group. The physical practice group practiced the musical sequence daily for two hours over a period of five days. The mental practice group sat in front of a piano and *imagined* playing the sequence and hearing it being played, also for two hours a day for five days. The brains of each individual in each group were monitored before the experiment, each day during their practicing, and following the experiment. At completion, both groups played the musical sequence while their accuracy was measured by a computer. Pascual-Leone discovered that after five days of practice—physical or mental—the brains in both groups of people had the same changes in motor signals to the muscles. The participants in the group who simply imagined themselves playing the sequence were nearly as accurate as the group who physically practiced. This study shows that simply *imagining* ourselves doing an activity can not only change the physical structures in our brain and lead to the learning of a new physical skill with minimal physical practice, but also that *imagining* can enhance the accuracy of our physical performance of that activity. (Alvaro Pascual-Leone, N. Dang, L. G. Cohen, J. P. Brasil-Neto, A. Cammarota, and M. Hallett, "Modulation of Muscle Responses Evoked by Transcranial Magnetic Stimulation During the Acquisition of New Fine Motor Skills," *Journal of Neurophysiology*, 74, no. 3, 1995: 1037–1045.)

EXERCISE: Mental Health Break

Research from the Institute of HeartMath shows that experiencing pleasure or appreciation releases endorphins into the body, and five minutes of experiencing positive feelings is enough to counteract the toxic chemicals released during hours of stress! Within your brain, you easily have five minutes worth of pleasant memories. Flex your imagination muscles and heal your body by spending just five minutes a day recalling these great memories. Make it a regular part of your daily routine, maybe while commuting to work or brushing your teeth. Five pleasant minutes first thing in the morning will set you up for an endorphin-filled day. Five minutes at night will ensure a wonderful night's sleep!

morning cartoons when Mighty Mouse or Batman wins the day! Rationally, we know that movies, books, and cartoons are not within the reality of our daily lives. Yet, our brains and physiology still respond almost as fully as if they are events occurring to us in our own living rooms. A brain that can get your entire physiology to respond to a cartoon is definitely plastic enough to accept the new stories and beliefs you choose for it!

Visualization and Performance

For centuries, philosophers and psychologists have talked about our innate ability to focus our brainpower to produce good in our lives. But the power of visualization and mental training first gained scientific credibility and public attention in the realm of athletics and the pursuit of peak performance. During the Olympics of 1976, the Soviet Union won more gold medals than any other country and East Germany nearly swept the field in swimming. The results were so stunning that researchers like Charles Garfield (who coined the term "peak performance" in 1986 during his work on the Apollo mission) arranged to meet with Soviet trainers and athletes.

He discovered that these countries had been emphasizing mental training for their Olympic athletes.

> Nothing happens unless first a dream.
>
> —*Carl Sandburg*

In one study, athletes were divided into four groups: Group 1 trained physically only. Group 2 spent 25 percent of their training time using mental exercises and 75 percent of their time in physical training. Group 3 divided their training time evenly, 50 percent mental and 50 percent physical. Group 4 devoted 75 percent of their training to mental practice and 25 percent to physical. Group 4 improved their performance significantly over the improvement Group 3 experienced. Group 3's performance had improved much more than Group 2 and Group 1. Group 1, with no mental training, showed the least improvement of all groups. The athletes who spent the most time on mental training had focused their brains toward achieving the results they desired. As always, their brains used their power to support the beliefs conditioned into them.

Since those early days, mental training for peak performance has been used in many different arenas, such as in business, the arts, health, goal

Researchers from the University of Iowa in Iowa City conducted an experiment that proved that when you imagine strengthening your muscles, you actually strengthen them! Researchers divided thirty subjects into two groups—one group exercised a finger muscle for five sessions per week for four weeks. The second group simply imagined exercising a finger muscle while also imagining a voice cheering them on by shouting, "Harder, harder, harder!" for the same period. At the end of the four weeks, subjects who had participated in the physical exercise increased their muscle strength by 30 percent. However, subjects who used their imagination *alone* ended up increasing their muscular strength by 22 percent! (G. Yue and K. Cole, "Strength Increases From the Motor Program: Comparison of Training with Maximal Voluntary and Imagined Muscle Contractions," *Journal of Neurophysiology*, 67, no. 5, 1992: 1114–1123.)

setting, and education. You've undoubtedly heard motivational speakers encouraging us to "visualize a positive result" in everything from hitting a golf ball to finding true love. The power in visualization is that strong images fed to the brain can reprogram its neuropathways, causing the brain to produce those positive results. But it has to be done correctly to be effective.

Visualization vs. Imagination

When I work with clients to plant new stories into the brain, I prefer the term *imagination* over visualization. Many of us do not consider ourselves to be visual, and asking someone to visualize can be confusing. Is it supposed to look like a movie in our minds? Does it have to be in color? Some clients get overly analytical about visual detail: "But if it's a June wedding, maybe it will be too hot. What about mosquitoes? Would gardenias still be in bloom? If not, what kind of flower . . . ?"

Our brains don't respond to detailed visualizations so much as to the emotional and feeling components in the experience of imagination. When we feel nervous for the movie heroine being chased by the killer, it is not because the picture is so clear but because we throw ourselves *into* the picture. We imagine ourselves being chased. We relate to the panic and terror our heroine feels. Though we sit in the safety of our living rooms, we are caught up in the drama on the screen, and our brains and bodies respond accordingly. It has nothing to do with what furniture our heroine encounters or the color of her carpets. It's our ability to fully *imagine* the experience itself.

We're Imagination Pros

Clear visualization may be beyond some of us, but all of us are well-versed in using our imagination. For instance, we tap that vast power of imagination whenever we worry. The definition of worry is "to feel anxious about something unpleasant that may or may not happen." When we worry, we activate our entire system based on an event that has not occurred yet and may not ever occur. Yet the emotions we feel and physical sensations we experience are real.

> Worry is like a rocking chair: It gives you something to do, but it doesn't get you anywhere.
>
> —*Erma Bombeck*

What happens when your daughter doesn't come home when you expect her and she doesn't call? Especially if this is a rare occurrence, most of us begin to worry and make up a story about it: "Maybe she's lost or hurt. Maybe she's been in an accident. Maybe she's been kidnapped!" Even though no real event has happened, your brain will signal your physiology to respond to the worry-story you're telling it. You experience the full-blown anxiety,

EXERCISE: **Taking Charge of Worry**

Worry is one of those counterproductive activities that many of us fall into. Worry is often based on conditioned beliefs that have little to do with the situation at hand. More often than not, our worry turns out to be for naught—what we fear never takes place. Yet we waste precious moments of our lives in unwarranted anxiety. And in those rare times when the events we fear *do* occur, the emotional state of worry does not prepare us to respond effectively.

So the next time worry comes to your doorstep: Pause. Breathe deeply, using the belly breathing rhythm of Chapter 5.

As you continue breathing, inhale and experience the feeling and physical sensations of worry: your jittery stomach and pounding heartbeat, your racing mind. As you exhale, allow these feelings to be released.

After several breaths, ask yourself these questions:
- Do I really know what is happening?
- Could there be another explanation?
- Is there any action I can take to affect the outcome of this situation right now?

Now, ask yourself: Is this a familiar pattern of worrying? If so, it's likely that a conditioned pattern of worry has been activated.

fear, and panic. Your body may feel tense or you may experience a rush of adrenaline preparing your body to act. And when your daughter waltzes in thirty minutes later oblivious to your concern, often anxiety channels into rage and you're fully prepared to strangle her! All of this activity and reaction was based on something that never occurred.

We also use our power of imagination when we speculate about people or events. The definition of speculate is "to conjecture about something based on incomplete facts or information." In other words, we don't know what's going on so we make it up.

In my experience, women are especially good at speculating about relationships. Most of my female clients can relate to the example of not getting a phone call from someone after a first date. Speculation over why the phone doesn't ring and the emotion our speculation elicits can be endless: "Maybe he is too shy to call" (compassion, empathy). "Maybe I said something to offend him" (embarrassment, shame). "Maybe he thinks he's too good for me" (anger, resentment). "Maybe he just didn't find me attractive" (sadness, hurt).

Men are equally good at speculation, as reflected in the story about the salesman whose car broke down in the middle of the night on a country road. Spotting a light in a farmhouse at a distance, the salesman begins to walk through the fields to get assistance. And as he walks, he speculates: "Maybe they go to bed early because they are farmers. Maybe I'll wake everyone up and they'll be angry. Maybe they won't want to help me or lend me the tools I need. Maybe they think city folks are stupid." After several minutes of this internal dialogue, he finally gets to the farmhouse. And when the farmer flings open the door, the salesman hollers, "Keep your damn jack!"

If you can speculate or worry, you have a highly developed imagination and you know how to use it. Now the trick is to use this skill in ways that serve you.

Let's Pretend

As children, most of us loved to pretend. We didn't pretend little things. We pretended greatness or at least levels beyond where we were. A ferocious pirate sailing the high seas. A beautiful strong princess saving the castle. A famous detective solving a crime. An important surgeon saving a life. Whether we used our own bodies or our dolls or action figures to pretend, we didn't just tell the stories. We threw ourselves into them and felt heroic, brilliant, brave, and extraordinary.

It's not just children who are good at pretending. Years ago, a friend of mine taught a martial art called Aikido. She often used an exercise where she asked newer students to pretend to be black belts. "While advanced students demonstrated a technique, I asked the new students to watch them and try to *feel* what the advanced students seemed to feel as they performed." After observing for a few minutes, the new students were asked to "pretend to be

> Fiction is the truth inside the lie.
>
> —*Stephen King*

EXERCISE: Black Belt Moments

Think of a characteristic that you desire for yourself. Maybe you wish to be faster on your feet verbally or to be more expressive around people. Maybe you'd like to be more assertive or more flirtatious. Whatever characteristic you choose, find people in your environment who exemplify that trait to you. Observe their posture, how they walk and hold themselves. Notice their quality of voice and rhythm of speech. Notice their facial expressions and hand gestures. Rather than trying to mimic what you see, use your observation and imagination to feel what these others might be feeling.

As you move through your day, call up that feeling. Walk down the hallway with the stride of the person who has your desired characteristic. Interact with the grocery clerk as you sense your example person might interact. Let yourself pretend to be that person. And as you do, take note of how pretending to be the other person feels different from "being yourself."

> Do not quench your inspiration and your imagination; do not become the slave of your model.
>
> —*Vincent van Gogh*

black belts" as they performed the technique they had been shown. She tells me that the results were amazing: Gawky, awkward white belts were suddenly graceful and strong, not technically perfect but centered and powerful. "The funniest thing was that when we stopped our pretending exercise, the new students reverted immediately to being off-balance and clumsy." But in the moments of pretending, their brains organized their bodies to perform according to their black belt fantasy.

Using our imaginations consciously and constructively, incorporating deep breathing and full experience of feelings, is critical to the process of rewiring our brains. These are tools that you have naturally, but there are some keys to make them work for you.

Positive Focus

We often use the power of our imaginations against ourselves. We speculate or worry about what we *do not* want, rather than what we *do* want. We anticipate an important meeting and imagine all the things that could go wrong. We begin a new relationship and fret about our own (or the other person's) imperfections. Our what-ifs are filled with everything we would like to avoid: "What if she betrays me? What if we miss that deadline? What if the economy gets worse?" By focusing on what we do not want, we are actually wiring our brains to *expect and create* the reality we want to prevent.

When athletes work with visualization and mental training, they don't spend time imagining what they *don't* want. They don't imagine falling off the beam or hitting a turn out of rhythm. They don't imagine stumbling off the block or missing the target. These athletes imagine doing their moves perfectly and accurately, with strength and grace. Imagining a great performance causes the brain to signal blood flow, muscles, breathing, and all

In 1980, sports psychologist Richard Suinn tested the psychoneuromuscular theory, that is, how visualization and imaging help to enhance the performance of athletes training for peak performance. This theory states that during the imaging of an activity, the brain sends out similar signals to the body as it does when the individual is actually engaging the activity, and thereby establishes a mental blueprint of what is needed to perform the activity. This blueprint makes the activity easier to execute and enhances the athletes' ability to perform. Suinn used an imagery technique, visuo-motor behavior rehearsal (VMBR), that he developed, and attached electrodes from an electromyograph (EMG) to the legs of a skier to measure the physiological response of the skier while he visualized himself racing downhill. Suinn discovered that the physiological responses of the skier while visualizing were almost identical to those when he actually skied the course. Suinn states, "By the time he finished the psychological rehearsal of the downhill race, his EMG recordings almost mirrored the course itself." (Richard M. Suinn, *Psychology of Sports: Methods and Applications*, Minneapolis: Burgess, 1980, 306–315.)

physical systems to conform to this image of excellence. Each time the image is called up, the athlete's brain and physiology get to rehearse, responding more quickly and fully with each rehearsal.

Many of my clients start out with a clear sense of what they don't want: "I don't want to procrastinate so much at work." "I don't want to freeze up whenever I speak publicly." "I don't want to yell at my kids all the time." "I don't want to be overweight." Often when I encourage them to think of what they *do* want, it still comes out as a version of what they *don't* want: "I want to stop procrastinating at work." "I want to be less frozen whenever I speak publicly." "I want to avoid yelling at my kids." "I want to lose weight." An image that begins with those statements will still focus on what is *un*wanted and that is what the brain and physiology will rehearse.

Effective beginning statements must focus only on what *is* wanted. Using the examples above, good starting statements might be: "I am effective on the job, working efficiently and with great focus. I get things done quickly

EXERCISE: **What Are You Rehearsing?**

Unintentionally, many of us rehearse what we do *not* wish to happen. We think about an upcoming event or interaction and imagine the worst that could happen rather than the best. By doing so, we train our brains to fail.

Over the next week, pay attention to your normal mental rehearsals. When you hunt for a parking space, are you thinking about how limited parking is? When you head to the gym, are you telling yourself how uncomfortable and boring your workout will be? In thinking about an upcoming meeting, are you playing out the worst that could happen in your mind? If so, you are using the same techniques professional athletes use— but in the opposite direction!

Next time you catch yourself mentally training to fail, see if you can turn it around: Imagine abundant parking, easy and fun workouts, brilliant meetings with great outcomes. As you get more proficient in this, you'll find that not only is your experience more pleasant, but your brain will direct itself to produce the results you envision.

and always meet my deadlines." "I enjoy public speaking and feel confident as I deliver my message." "I am calm and centered with my children, handling all situations with wisdom and love." "I am slim and healthy. I love and appreciate my body."

Present Focus

As we rehearse the brain, the new story we feed it needs to be in the *present*. "Someday my prince will come" or "someday my ship will come in" are fantasies that elicit hope and longing. If you use future-based images and statements, your brain and physiology practice *yearning for a future* event rather the *experience of the event made manifest*. Your brain and body get really proficient at *craving* a lover rather than the feeling of being loved and the warmth of a lover's embrace. They become expert at the *wistful desire* for wealth rather than the freedom and security wealth might bring.

Keeping your image in the present applies even when your goal or desire has an obvious time element attached to it. If your goal is to obtain a graduate degree, you will want your brain to rehearse the joy and pride of your

> Don't think of your goals, think from your goals.
>
> —*Mark Victor Hansen*

graduation ceremony along with the enjoyment you feel and brilliance you show as you take classes toward it. If your goal is to weigh forty pounds less than you do today, you should imagine yourself at that perfect weight and how it feels physically and emotionally in the present, along with how great it feels to exercise daily and eat good foods in healthy portions.

Beyond Words

Your conscious imagining may start with a statement like, "I feel confident in social situations." But a mere statement has little power. When you worried about your daughter being late, you didn't just sit back and think, "Hmm. Maybe she's been in an accident. That's interesting." No! You threw yourself into it, maybe feeding your anxiety with details and additional fears. You added guilt or anger to the mix. The experience was powerful because you stepped into the worry fully enough to get your brain and body involved.

Remember when you pretended to be a pirate on the seven seas? You didn't just say, "I'm a pirate." You incorporated your whole system and stepped into *being* a pirate: You felt ferocious and brave like a pirate. You walked with the swaggering, masterful stride of a pirate and wielded your sword with a pirate's wild abandon. You gave your fantasy context and specific situations. You imagined yourself on a rolling ship during a ferocious storm or fighting a fierce battle on a sunny tropical beach. You felt your muscles strain against the sails, or the quick movement of your feet as you sidestepped your opponent's sword. You felt your heart pound and the determined set of your jaw.

> Visualize doing the activity, and feel it kinesthetically, and hear the accompanying sounds, smell the accompanying odors, and, if possible, taste the accompanying tastes. Incorporating as many senses as possible makes the image more real and life-like. This is important. ... The brain cannot easily distinguish between a real and an imagined event.
>
> —*Anees Sheikh*

Similarly, when we use our imaginations to reprogram our brains, we need to throw ourselves into the experience and get all of our senses involved to make an impact.

Start Easy

As you begin feeding your brain new stories and images, you may want to start small. If you have been conditioned to believe that you are homely, your brain may not buy into an image of you becoming *People* magazine's "Sexiest Person Alive." If you've never jogged in your life, your brain might be understandably skeptical about winning an Olympic Gold Medal in the four hundred meters. Stretch your brain slowly and expand your images as you grow more confident.

For example, if your desire is to feel more self-assured, your beginning statement might be "I feel confident in social situations" (positive, present, specific). The context of your image might be walking into a crowded room of people that you know. (Later, as you feel more comfortable, you might switch to a room full of strangers.) As you imagine entering the room, sense your posture as comfortable and relaxed, your walk as self-assured. Your gaze would be welcoming and warm. You might feel eager to connect with people, poised in conversation. Imagine specific interactions with people and their positive response to you. You are a black belt in social situations!

> Everything you can imagine is real.
>
> —*Pablo Picasso*

Not only does mental imagery enhance athletic performance, but it has been shown to enhance intrinsic motivation as well. The University of Western Ontario conducted an investigation into the effects of mental imagery on the motivation and willingness to practice a golf putting task with thirty-nine volunteers who had played two or fewer rounds of golf. These beginner golfers were randomly assigned to two groups: an imagery group or a no-imagery group. For three sessions, both groups were taught how to hit golf balls. The imagery group also participated in an imagery training session designed for this specific golf skill. Another three sessions were devoted to practicing. Researchers found that "subjects in the imagery group spent significantly more time practicing the golf putting task than subjects in the no-imagery group, and they set higher goals for themselves and had more realistic self-expectations." These results indicate that mental imagery could be used to enhance motivation to practice and to persist in practicing, and that imagery may be seen as a valuable motivational tool. (Kathleen A. Martin and Craig R. Hall, "Using Mental Imagery to Enhance Intrinsic Motivation," *Journal of Sport and Exercise Psychology*, 17, 1995: 54–69.)

What if your goal is to reduce conflict with your children? You might begin with "My interactions with my children are warm and loving, calm and consistent." In the beginning, you might imagine a comfortable family setting, sharing a holiday meal together or quietly enjoying a television program. (In later stages, you can practice with the scene where your children have set fire to the garage!) Sense how relaxed and comfortable you feel physically. Experience the loving feelings and thoughts you have toward your children in that moment. Imagine the open, calm conversation you have with one another, the easy laughter you share.

Not Just a Daydream

Walter Mitty has given imagination a bad rap! In the story of Walter Mitty, the main character avoids the pain and boredom of his life by daydreaming of being a variety of great heroes. Using imagination in that manner might

EXERCISE: Create Your Image

This exercise will be most effective if you set aside at least ten minutes to do it and find a quiet place where you will not be disturbed. Choose one change you would like from your list of desires or goals. Begin by crafting a brief statement of what you want. Remember, it should be positive, in present tense, and somewhat specific.

Next imagine that this statement is already true and imagine yourself within an applicable situation. If your goal is financial stability, imagine yourself happily paying bills or having a fun shopping spree. If weight loss is your desire, imagine appreciating your body as you try on new clothes or showing up to your high school reunion at the weight you were when you graduated.

Stay with your imagined scene for several minutes and let it unfold with action or new detail. Most importantly, bask in the way it feels in your body and emotions. By doing so, you are focusing your brain, allowing it to rehearse for the new reality you desire.

be entertaining, but it will not rewire the brain any more than watching an afternoon matinee. To get lasting effects and significant improvement in performance, Soviet athletes participated in mental *training* for the Olympics, not mental vacations. They used their imaginations intentionally, carefully crafting the images they wished their brains to adopt and incorporating breathing and feelings. They brought full focus to mental training sessions, taking the process seriously. These athletes were consistent and persistent with their mental training.

That said, using your imagination to rewire your brain should be fun! The images that you create to support your goals and desires should give you pleasure. Each time you train your brain using your imagination, it should feel as good as stepping into a hot shower or a bubble bath. Your imagination sessions should leave you feeling excited, energized, and vibrant.

> If at first, the idea is not absurd, there is no hope for it.
>
> —*Albert Einstein*

Can't Imagine It?

When clients have trouble really imagining their desired results, there are a few possible causes. Some of my clients discover that they do not really want what they think they want! They have been so attuned to the expectations and aspirations of others that they lose sight of what they truly desire. In those cases, trying to imagine something they don't really want is fighting with their internal wisdom. For these clients, our first step is to discover what *they* desire—not what their parents want or society wants, not what their spouses expect.

> Your vision will become clear only when you look into your heart. Who looks outside, dreams. Who looks inside, awakens.
>
> —*Carl Jung*

For other clients, the realization of their goal seems completely foreign, totally unlike any previous experience. If you've never been in an argument without exploding in verbal rage, it may be hard to conjure up an image of

---

EXERCISE: **Self-Discovery**

If you suspect that some of your existing goals are not really yours, you might find it helpful to answer the following questions about them:

- Who wants this goal more, me or _____ ?
- Whose idea was this in the first place?
- After I attain this goal, how will I feel? How will others feel? How will my feeling be affected by what others feel?
- If my family and friends were not excited about this goal, would I be?
- Will I have to give up another desire for this one? Which do I really prefer?

What dreams have I given up because they didn't meet the approval of my family, culture, friends, spouse?

Remember that your brain will support whatever you program into it. Make sure that your new conscious empowering beliefs are the ones you really want.

> The pages are still blank, but there is a miraculous feeling of the words being there, written in invisible ink and clamoring to become visible.
>
> —*Vladimir Nabokov*

calm, cool, and collected. If your financial situation has always been a problem, you may not really know how it feels to be financially stable and solvent. If you break into a sweat just thinking about writing, it might be hard to imagine having a successful, fun career as an author.

If your new image is totally out of your experience, use the black belt technique: observe someone who is, does, or has what you desire. As you observe, try to sense how they feel and think. Note their posture, breathing, facial expressions, their actions, their speech. If there is no one around you to observe, try reading or watching biographies of those with the experience you lack. Even fictional characters can give you some clues.

Finally, your new desire or goal may very well be in complete opposition to your prior conditioning. If your imagination is being blocked by a strong conditioned belief or story, you may need to work with your old story to soften its hold or cleanse it from your system (see Chapter 7). The lack of cleansing is often what makes positive affirmations ineffective: Every time you affirm and try to imagine "I am a great success," your strong conditioning responds with, "Yeah, right, Loser!" The "Loser" experience is ingrained and much more compelling than a few positive words or a wistful image. In the next chapters, I'll show you how

> Sometimes dreams are wiser than waking.
>
> —*Black Elk*

to cleanse that old conditioning so that your brain is receptive and ready to be carved with the neuropathways you choose consciously, the ones that support your desires.

Chapter 7

The Power of Acknowledgment: Face It or Get Chased by It

Do you remember the film *Groundhog Day?* In it, Bill Murray plays a character who relives a certain day, February 2, over and over, ad nauseum. Every morning, his alarm clock awakens him with the same tune at the same time in the same room. Throughout the day, he meets the same people and same circumstances. At first, he has some fun with this and the foreknowledge it brings. But as time goes on, reenacting this one day drives him crazy and he becomes desperate to break free of the relentless repetition. But he can't. No matter what he does or says, he remains condemned to the same rut.

Many of us have felt the same way, that the days of our lives are an endless string of déjà vu. Despite our best intentions, we end up reliving the

> In just refusing to retreat from something one gains the strength of two men.
>
> —*Shungaku*

same old patterns that are contrary to our best interests. We eat in ways that are unhealthy and place ourselves in dead-end jobs. We pick fights with our parents and rack up too much credit card debt. We hesitate to express ourselves and deny our talents, our brilliance.

By now, it should be clear to you that these oft-repeated, limiting patterns are part of your conditioning and have been hardwired into your brain. It should also be clear that you can consciously rewire this conditioning to transform your life. Though the science behind this rewiring or reprogramming is complex, the steps you need to take to work with your brain effectively are simple and straightforward. If you want to avoid living your life as just another Groundhog Day, the first step is to acknowledge and cleanse your old conditioning.

You Are *Not* Your Conditioning

Though the first step is simple, my clients often resist it. One client explained her resistance to digging into her conditioned stories and their underlying feelings this way: "What if I look deeply inside and I don't like the me that I see?"

When we've spent our lives operating and reacting according to our conditioned beliefs, it's easy to identify *with* them and *as* them. "That's just my personality." "That's just who I am." "It's in my DNA." "I'm just wired that way." Though your conditioning shows how you are currently *wired*, it's *not* who you are. Your conditioned stories and reactions were handed to you or invented by you unconsciously. They may be petty or ugly or painful, but they are no more *you* than a mole on your shoulder.

And just like that mole on your shoulder, it makes no sense to feel guilt, shame, or self-criticism about your conditioning. It just is what it is, part of the human condition. We all have limiting conditioned beliefs and reactions that run our lives. It's unlikely that yours are worse than your neighbor's or your spouse's. The only thing "bad" about them is that they have kept you from what you desire.

> Let the world know you as you are, not as you think you should be.
>
> —*Fanny Brice*

My husband and I have found a way to lighten up our approach to our conditioned reactions by affectionately naming them The Monster. Somehow, using this name helps us remain clear that The Monster is not who we really are and certainly does not represent the way we wish to interact with one another or with the world. Whenever one of us acts out using an old negative pattern, we stop ourselves and say, "Whoa! Looks like The Monster has come out to play!" By acknowledging The Monster but not getting caught up in its antics, we have the choice to feed it or send it on its way!

One of the goals of the step of acknowledgment is to establish that separation between you and your conditioning. The Monster is not me and it's not you. But if we want to keep it from running the show, we first have to pay some attention to it before we can take charge.

> Be who you are and say what you feel, because those who mind don't matter and those who matter don't mind.
>
> —*Dr. Seuss*

From Monologue to Dialogue

Have you ever tried to have a discussion with someone who is so enamored with or adamant about their own opinions that you can't get a word in edgewise? And when you try to offer a contrary point of view, that person pumps up the volume and becomes even more vehement to drown you out? This is how your conditioned beliefs, a.k.a. The Monster, respond when you try to introduce different beliefs.

Your conditioned beliefs are certain that they are correct. They have years of proof to offer and can cite specific examples to reinforce their validity. They are firmly ensconced in your brain, emotions, and body, and

> If you shut your door to all errors, truth will be shut out.
>
> —*Rabindranath Tagore*

have probably been calling the shots for much of your life. Sending your new fledgling beliefs into battle against your powerful, old, entrenched conditioned beliefs is like sending David into battle against Goliath—without his slingshot!

Behind Your Back

You also can't simply ignore these conditioned beliefs. Even if you turn your back on The Monster and refuse to acknowledge its existence, these beliefs are hardwired in and still control your physiology. Your brain will continue to do everything in its power to support your conditioned beliefs, creating ingenious ways to sabotage your efforts to change.

A friend of mine, Linda, is a golfer who was determined to break 100 a couple of years ago. She bought new clubs for more distance, worked to improve her swing, studied course management, and learned a steadier grip for putting. She had everything in place physically and felt pretty confident as she stepped out to play her first round that spring. It all went according to plan until the eighteenth hole when she realized that her score to that point was only 89, the best round of her life! She just needed to shoot 10 or less on the last hole to reach her goal.

But her brain was still convinced that Linda was not then and never would be a good golfer and was determined to prove it. She shot a 12.

An elderly acquaintance of mine, Roy, had always dreamed of being a commercial artist. His parents were skeptical of the idea, instilling in him the fear of becoming a "starving artist," and encouraging the more practical pursuit of construction work. But in the early 1940s, the Disney Studios were expanding rapidly and sent out a call for cartoonists. On a whim, Roy submitted his work and was granted an interview. Excited about the opportunity, Roy put together his portfolio and took the bus all the way from Michigan to Burbank, California.

And as he stepped off the bus, he broke his leg and ended up in the hospital, missing his appointment and his big opportunity.

I would argue that there was more than bad luck behind both of these stories. Linda's brain was imbedded with the conditioned belief that she's not the athletic type, and her brain directed her body to prove it. Roy's brain made sure that he was protected from the uncertain life of a starving artist by literally tripping him up! Because these conditioned beliefs were not acknowledged and cleansed, The Monster still maintained its power, despite Linda and Roy's strong desires to the contrary.

Out of Sight, Still in Mind

Of course, most of us never realized that we had limiting beliefs wired into our brains in the first place, much less that they wielded such power! So how can we recognize that we have them? Your first clue might be when you've tried multiple times to make a change in your life but remain unsuccessful. As with Linda and Roy, your brain is sabotaging your efforts.

You may also hear contradictory voices in your head. Your statement of desire is consistently followed by a strong *but*. "I want to be in a relationship, *but* people can hurt you when they get close." "I'd like to be in management, *but* I might lose all my friends at work." "I'd like to be slimmer, *but* I'd have to give up all the pleasure and comfort of food." "I'd like to stop yelling at my kids, *but* if I did, they would just run amuck." The statement after *but* is The Monster, your limiting conditioned belief, talking.

It may look like a wreck, but go at it as though it were an opportunity, a challenge. If you bring love to that moment—not discouragement—you will find the strength is there. Any disaster you can survive is an improvement in your character, your stature, and your life! What a privilege! This is when the spontaneity of your own nature will have a chance to flow.

—*Joseph Conrad*

This limiting belief may also show up as a feeling with no statement of rationale attached: Whenever you are attracted to someone, you feel awkward and shy. Every time you think of applying for a management position, you feel anxious. When you start a diet, you feel depressed. Whenever you remain silent regarding your children's inappropriate behavior, you feel panicky. Beneath those feelings lies your limiting belief.

Acknowledgment and Cleansing

As mentioned earlier, the first step of the rewiring process is acknowledgement. Remember that emotions are feelings that have become firmly attached to a conditioned story and emotions supply power to your hardwiring to keep it in place. In this first step, you acknowledge the conditioned belief or story that blocks you, then take a few moments to acknowledge and experience the feelings associated with it. Then you use your breath to release the conditioned story and feelings, to soften their hold on you and clear the path for new, positive beliefs to be carved into your brain.

Acknowledging your limiting belief does not mean getting into a huge dialogue with it, describing it or its history in excruciating detail. The intention is not to argue or agree with The Monster, simply to acknowledge it. When you are in a confrontation with someone, have you ever tried calmly acknowledging their point of view to defuse the situation? "So, you're saying that you feel I've overstepped my bounds? That I should have asked you first before proceeding?" Acknowledging your conditioned story will have the same effect and should have the same quality: no blame, no accusations, no judgment. Just a calm statement of what The Monster believes to be true.

As you acknowledge the limiting story, do so with the sense that it is merely a belief, a perspective, an opinion. No matter how real it has felt or appeared in the past, this belief is not fact. It is a false truth of your conditioning. It has no validity beyond that which your brain has given it. And

UCLA psychiatrist Jeffery Schwartz conducted a study that provided hard evidence that regular mental practice can alter and enhance brain function. Working with patients suffering from obsessive-compulsive disorder (OCD), Schwartz investigated whether the positive behavioral changes he was seeing in his patients would be accompanied by structural changes in their brains. Eighteen medication-free OCD patients, with moderate to severe symptoms, were given brain scans before and after ten weeks of treatment. During the ten weeks, each time a patient experienced an onslaught of an obsessive thought they would say to themselves something like, "It's not me. It's my OCD." This acknowledgment allowed the patient to separate themselves from the problem and see it as a product of a faulty brain circuit. Then they were guided to consciously refocus their attention on a positive, more adaptive behavior, or as Schwartz puts it, "substitute a 'good (pattern) for a 'bad' one." Results showed that twelve patients had significant improvements in behavioral symptoms and their brain scans showed significantly improved functioning. In other words, the obsessive-compulsive pattern had been broken in these twelve patients, and this was accompanied by a reversal of the hyperactivity in specific brain regions associated with the disorder. (Jeffery M. Schwartz and S. Begley, *The Mind and the Brain: Neuroplasticity and the Power of Mental Force*, New York: Regan Books, 2002.)

if seeing this belief as false is too much for you to swallow initially, at least allow yourself to question its solidity.

Next, allow the feelings attached to this belief to arise, again without censorship or judgment. As feelings and emotions come to the surface, encourage them by noticing where they occur in your body and how your body responds. It might be tightness in the jaw, jittery stomach, or a hollow feeling in the chest. Describe these feelings to yourself to encourage them further. They might be sad, panicky, frightened, or lonely. Whatever they are, allow yourself to experience them fully.

As you stay with the experience of your feelings, allow them to increase in intensity—but do not add more storylines to them! For example, if the feeling is "lonely," do not inventory every circumstance within which you have felt lonely, who was involved, what you did: "This feels like the time in third grade when Rosie Turner had a party and didn't invite me, and I sat all day crying with my Barbie doll, and my brother laughed at me and called me a wimp and I . . ." The point is to stay focused on the pure feeling itself.

Finally, use belly breathing and your imagination to unplug this story and its feelings from your physiology. Inhale deeply to the count of four as you've practiced, and use your imagination to focus the incoming breath on the feeling and where it is felt in your body. Let your breath gently surround it and soften it. As you exhale to the count of six, imagine that feeling releasing its hold, leaving your body by riding your breath as it is expelled. Repeat this process several times until you sense that the feeling has softened or disappeared.

It's important during this breathing and imagining stage to remain focused but gentle. Your breath is not a SWAT team swooping into your system to exterminate unwanted conditioned beliefs and feelings! Your brain would perceive that as threatening and would activate survival mechanisms to fend off attempts to rewire it. But your deep breathing will activate your

EXERCISE: Acknowledge and Cleanse

Set yourself up in a quiet, comfortable place where you will not be disturbed for at least ten minutes. Choose a conditioned belief that you wish to release.

Acknowledge your limiting belief, recognizing it as a false truth, and allow its accompanying feeling to surface. Allow yourself to fully experience the feeling, noticing where that feeling resides in your body and describing it to yourself.

Begin your slow, deep belly breathing. Inhale with a focus on the feeling within. Exhale and allow the feeling to release. Imagine your breath gently surrounding the feeling as you inhale. Imagine your feeling relaxing and leaving your body as you exhale. Do this for several breaths or as long as you can until you start to feel the shift within.

natural relaxation response, signaling your brain that all is well as you calm and coax old patterns to release their grip.

Feeling Not So Groovy

On paper, this process sounds pretty simple, right? But many of us avoid acknowledging or facing negative conditioned beliefs and stories because they don't feel good—and only a masochist chooses to spend time intentionally feeling rotten! Most of us would choose good feelings, or even no feelings at all, over bad feelings. The feelings and emotions that help carve limiting beliefs into our brains are often unpleasant: anger, fear, sadness, grief, shame, guilt. When we bring a limiting belief to consciousness to face The Monster, the rotten feeling associated with it pops up as well.

Here's the good news: simply allowing yourself to fully experience the negative feeling associated with your conditioned belief helps release it! Here's the bad news: most of us have not been taught how to do this. We've been taught to keep a stiff upper lip, keep plodding ahead, cope, work around it, resist wallowing. Theoretically, we may recognize that negative feelings are a natural part of life. But on a visceral level, we don't trust them: Will I lose control if I allow that anger to be felt? If I get into my sadness, will it be a miserable, tear-soaked, bottomless pit? If I face my shame or guilt, will I ever be able to look myself in the eye? If I feel that fear, will I become frozen and unable to act?

> Courage is not the absence of fear, but rather the judgment that something else is more important than fear.
>
> —*Ambrose Redmoon*

With a little experience, getting into these difficult feelings is not so scary. Any discomfort is far outweighed by the opening created when limiting beliefs are released, an opening that allows new, positive beliefs to become wired into the brain, which in turn causes your brain to support these new life-expanding beliefs. But if that is not enough motivation for

A study conducted at the Department of Psychology at Rosalind Franklin University of Medicine and Science provides evidence that the suppression of the emotion of anger is linked to the severity of chronic pain. Researchers studied fifty-eight individuals with chronic lower back pain. These individuals were assigned to one of two groups—suppression or nonsuppression of anger. Both groups were asked to perform a mental task and then were harassed by another participant. The researchers found that "attempts to suppress emotions during provocation produced feelings of anger greater than what was felt by patients who were also harassed but did not try to suppress." Additionally, the suppression group experienced greater pain intensity during the task and exhibited more pain behaviors than individuals who were not suppressing their anger. The researcher concluded that this study "contributes to establishing a causal connection between the tendency to suppress anger and the worsening of clinical pain." (John W. Burns et al., "Effects of Anger Suppression on Pain Severity and Pain Behaviors Among Chronic Pain Patients: Evaluation of an Ironic Process Model," *Health Psychology,* 27, no. 5, September 2008: 645–652.)

you, let me just point out that unexperienced feelings are dangerous to your health!

Suppressed Emotion

When feelings or emotions are suppressed and stuffed into hidden corners of your psyche, they also become lodged in some part of your physiology. The result can be chronic pain, body stiffness, fatigue, and stress-related diseases such as hypertension. You may not be conscious of the suppressed emotion that still lurks in your physiology, but your brain knows it is there and your brain knows that your intention is to keep it suppressed. So it helps you do so by building invisible cages and devising clever strategies to protect you from the unwanted feelings.

Take the example of unexperienced feelings of sadness. When we suppress sadness, we might find ourselves avoiding anything that would trigger the feeling: we won't watch sad movies, we can't listen to our friends' sad stories, we refuse to face difficult issues in a relationship. Each time a feeling of sadness gets close, our brains create distracting external reactions to keep it at bay: blaming others, verbal or emotional outbursts, nonproductive or self-destructive behaviors.

Or we may fall into the trap of retelling the conditioned story of our sadness. This carefully crafted story provokes a conditioned emotion (the original sadness might have been converted to anger, or feelings of being overwhelmed or ashamed) but keeps

> If you do not tell the truth about yourself you cannot tell it about other people.
>
> —*Virginia Woolf*

us on the surface of the experience. That familiar conditioned story never brings us to the heart, the real feeling of our original experience. On the flip side, our brains may repress the story altogether so that we do not recall the original experience accurately or even at all.

In all of these cases, we find ourselves emotionally limited and unable to maintain relationships beyond a certain level. We become not only unable to experience the depth of our painful feelings, but our positive feelings such as joy, passion, and love as well.

In order to heal and move on, it's important to really experience these suppressed feelings. We need to bring the underlying feelings of our conditioned stories to the surface, acknowledge them, and feel them within ourselves. In the first step of consciously rewiring our brains, acknowledgment, the most important thing to acknowledge is our feelings. Once the feelings have been acknowledged and experienced, we can use our breathing to release their hold on us. When we do so, our limiting conditioned beliefs begin to lose their power.

> "The horror of the moment," the King went on, "I shall never, never forget!" "You will though," said the Queen, "if you don't make a memorandum of it."
>
> —*Lewis Carroll, Through the Looking Glass*

Getting to the Feeling

There are numerous ways to get to the feeling attached to a conditioned belief. For many of us, just sitting quietly and thinking about the limiting belief brings its feelings to the surface. For others, it helps to talk it through with a close, trusted friend. Verbalizing and bouncing our thoughts off someone else often helps us get to the core of vague impressions. In either thinking or talking, the trick is to focus on unearthing the feeling. It's not necessary, and definitely not helpful, to spend any time on why a particular belief took hold, who was responsible, or how it has negatively affected your life. Acknowledging and releasing your feelings will help heal you; your analysis only carves the belief more deeply into your neuropathways.

> Things which matter most must never be at the mercy of things which matter least.
>
> —*Johann Wolfgang von Goethe*

For many of us, journaling is a process that uncovers feelings and insights that are not normally available through thinking or talking. When we write, we access the left side of the brain, which is associated with reason and analysis. This activity frees up the right side of the brain so we

Research carried out by Pennebaker and Beall at the Southern Methodist University showed that writing about personally traumatizing events has a beneficial effect on physical health and well-being. The researchers divided forty-six undergraduate students into groups that either wrote about superficial topics or the most traumatic experience of their life for fifteen minutes a day over the course of four days. The students who elaborated in their writings about personally traumatic events experienced relatively higher blood pressure and negative moods immediately following their writing sessions, but fewer health center visits in the six months following the experiment compared to the students who only wrote about trivial topics. (J. W. Pennebaker and S. K. Beall, "Confronting a Traumatic Event: Toward an Understanding of Inhibition and Disease," *Journal of Abnormal Psychology*, 95, 1985: 274–281.)

EXERCISE: Unearthing the Feeling

Start by writing down or stating what you desire.

Next, write or state the limiting conditioned belief or beliefs that stand in the way of this desire.

Then complete a few sentences using the structure, "My belief of _____ makes me feel _____."

For example:

- I want to write a book.
  * I can't write a book because I don't have enough time.
    » My belief that I don't have enough time makes me feel stressed and panicky.
  * I can't write a book because no one will want to read it.
    » My belief that no one will want to read it makes me feel hurt and unloved.
  * I can't write a book because I have nothing important to say.
    » My belief that I have nothing important to say makes me feel sad and hopeless.

As you uncover these emotions and feelings, give yourself some moments to fully experience them to discover how you feel emotionally and physically. Take some deep belly breaths, experiencing the emotion on the inhale and allowing it to release on the exhale.

can tap into intuition, creativity, and our feeling sense. When you write in your journal, avoid censoring yourself. This journal should be just for you. Don't worry about writing brilliantly or with grammatical correctness. Just let the writing flow, even if it seems to make little sense at all!

History Review

It also might help to recall an early experience that prompted or helped solidify the conditioned belief. As children, our feelings are more innocent, natural, and obvious. Use your imagination to put you back into the middle of that experience and to feel what you felt then. Whatever method you

EXERCISE: Ancient History

It isn't important to pinpoint the exact moment in time when your limiting belief first took hold. But it might be helpful to recall The Monster and its feelings somewhere in your childhood before those feelings could become suppressed. Use the following questions to help stimulate your memory:

- Can you think of a time when you didn't have this limiting belief? When did that change?
- As a child, did this belief apply to your school experience? Your friendships? Your family interactions?
- What dramatic or traumatic childhood experiences do you recall? Do any of them relate to this limiting conditioned belief?

Once you track down an early experience of The Monster, put yourself back in the scene and allow yourself to feel the emotions fully. Use your deep breathing to acknowledge and release the feelings.

EXERCISE: Catch It as It Comes Up

Our lives would improve tremendously simply by catching conditioned emotions as they pop up in daily life, experiencing them, and releasing them! This definitely takes some practice but it's worth it.

Over the course of a week or so, focus on one particular negative conditioned reaction that you would like to replace. For instance, perhaps you want to feel less defensive when criticized. Try to catch that feeling of defensiveness right when it pops up. Rather than responding to the criticism as you normally would, try an acknowledgement and cleansing miniprocess: Stop where you are, acknowledge the feeling silently with one word, such as *defensive,* and breathe deeply for thirty seconds or so until you sense that the feeling has relaxed. You may feel strange stopping to breathe mid-sentence, but the people around you will hardly notice—except for the fact that your responses to them will be more positive and constructive!

choose, the focus is to discover the under-lying feeling experientially. The intention is not to find someone or something to blame for the experience!

> If you don't release those who hurt you, you will begin to resemble them.
>
> —*Rick Warren*

You May Need Assistance

When feelings that we haven't experienced in the moment of a trauma lead to more serious conditions, such as anxiety disorder, major depression, or post-traumatic stress disorder, working with a professional counselor or therapist is advised. If your condition is not serious but you are unable or uncomfortable accessing certain feelings, you may be able to find a support group relevant to your issue.

> Never let yesterday use up too much of today.
>
> —*Will Rogers*

How Do I Use This?

In the next chapter, we will put the entire process together. I will show you step by step how to wire your brain with new neuropathways that support your goals and desires. But this step of acknowledging and cleansing can be powerful and life-transforming in and of itself. By consciously clearing old conditioned emotions and reactions, we put ourselves in the position of choice. The Monster is no longer in charge.

It takes some practice to incorporate the acknowledgment and cleansing process into daily life. I recommend that you set aside a few minutes every day to run through the process until it becomes familiar. For these practice times, choose small issues or large ones to work with, from the irritation you feel about your neighbor's dog barking to the terror you feel when facing a job interview.

> Begin at the beginning and go on till you come to the end; then stop.
>
> —*Lewis Carroll*

Finish each day and be done with it. You have done what you could. Some blunders and absurdities no doubt crept in; forget them as soon as you can. Tomorrow is a new day; begin it well and serenely and with too high a spirit to be encumbered with your old nonsense.

—*Ralph Waldo Emerson*

By regularly running the process, you are training yourself to quickly identify the feeling attached to a belief. You are training your physiology to experience those feelings and to release them. And you are getting to experience the clarity and freedom of consciously being in charge of your responses and actions.

Chapter 8

Pulling It All Together: Rewiring in a Nutshell

With what you have learned thus far, y ou have all the tools you need to effectively rewire your brain. By doing the exercises to this point, you've primed yourself to consciously recondition your beliefs with neuropathways that support your desires. As you do this, your brain will work to enforce your new truths as hard as it did to make sure your old, limiting beliefs became reality. Now that you've seen how powerfully your unconscious conditioning shapes your life, can you imagine what your new, life-affirming conditioning will do?

There are four basic steps to rewiring your brain—the Snap Out of it NOW! Method—and you've already experienced them in the previous chapters. In this chapter, we will put them all together. But please understand that this is not a magic pill, an instant fix. Your brain *will* be rewired and your life *will* be transformed, but only if you make a commitment to use this process consistently and persistently. This commitment to the process is actually a commitment to yourself and to your goals and desires.

Set Yourself Up

To work with the four-step Snap Out of it NOW! Method, find a quiet place where you will not be disturbed for ten to twenty minutes. Unplug your phone and tell your children that you're only available for life-threatening emergencies. Choose a time of day when you can be focused and relaxed. The ten minutes right before you have to rush out the door to get to work is probably not your best bet! Choose a comfortable chair and have your journal, notes, and this book with you. When you become familiar with the steps, you will be able to move through them by yourself. But in the beginning you may want to use the *Back in Charge!* CD to guide you.

1. **Acknowledge:** Acknowledge the specific conditioned belief that holds you back and acknowledge that it is not a fact but a false truth from your conditioning.
2. **Identify:** Be specific about this belief, and identify the feelings, emotions, and physical sensations that accompany it.
3. **Cleanse:** Unplug the feelings from your physiology by using your deep breathing and imagination.
4. **Insert a New Truth:** Condition your brain to a new truth by using your breathing and imagination.

Your Trigger

A trigger is a device used to get you back into the experience of your new belief quickly. It's usually a word that you associate with your new belief or story. A client who is a professional skier uses the word "supercalifragilisticexpialidocious." Whenever she says this word, she feels like a champion: strong, calm, prepared, focused. Another client uses "Donald Trump" whenever she goes into negotiations. The words bring her the feelings of confidence, clarity, and decisiveness. If you want to be calmer when dealing with your children, you might choose "Mother Teresa." To feel more comfortable in social situations, how about "warm connections" to help you feel relaxed and receptive?

> There is a law in psychology that if you form a picture in your mind of what you would like to be, and you keep and hold that picture there long enough, you will soon become exactly as you have been thinking.
>
> —*William James*

To create your trigger, find a word that expresses your new belief and helps to create the experience of your new image for yourself within. When you get to step four during your ten minute rewiring sessions, say that trigger word to yourself. Soon you'll find that your brain will recognize the connection between your trigger word and the experience of your new belief. It will produce the experience for you immediately and effortlessly.

> The future starts today, not tomorrow.
>
> —*Pope John Paul II*

EXERCISE: Create Your Trigger

If you have not already done so, create a trigger for yourself that will serve as a reminder. Some people use a rubber band around their wrists, enjoying the sensation of snapping themselves out of an old negative reaction before it becomes full blown. Many of us like the convenience of a word to jostle us toward our new belief. Whatever you choose, it should be a reminder that makes you feel good—not a slap on the wrist for bad behavior!

When you've chosen your trigger, practice with it during your quiet rewiring sessions. During step four when you use your breath and imagination to insert your new belief, speak (or snap) your trigger. This trains your brain to associate the experience of your new belief with your trigger.

Make It Stick

Your old conditioning has been powerful because of some very specific characteristics: (1) It was clear, detailed, and often repeated. (2) It involved all of the senses, which enabled it to become embedded in your physiology. (3) It had a strong emotional component—stories attached to strong feelings. These three characteristics not only kept the old conditioning firmly in place, but they were also critical to that neuropathway being carved in the first place.

The four steps are pretty simple. But to be successful, it's critical that we use those same three characteristics as we rewire the brain with our new conscious empowering beliefs.

Play It Again, Sam

The first characteristic of well-carved conditioned beliefs is repetition. A limiting conditioned belief becomes powerful because we have repeated it to ourselves over and over in various forms and in painful detail. Take the example of someone who has always had trouble losing weight. Her conditioned belief repeated itself and took many forms over the years: "I'm from the big side of the family. I'm just predisposed to be a little heavy." "Diets don't work for me. They are too restrictive and my lifestyle can't accommodate them." "Heavy people are happier. Skinny people tend to be tense and irritable." "People should just love me for who I am! I'm not going to lose weight just to attract a man." "Dieting takes all of the pleasure out of food. I want to enjoy life." And it was not just the things she said out loud or to herself. It was her repetitive actions as well: taking that second helping of dessert, skipping her exercise class, diving into comfort food after a hard day.

Have you ever heard that it takes twenty-one days to form a habit? It's the constant repetition that starts carving a neuropathway. Think about

University of Wisconsin–Madison researchers studied the potential of mental training in the form of meditation with an experiment to measure whether thousands of hours of meditation produce enduring changes in the brain. The study compared the brain functioning of eight Tibetan Buddhist meditators with that of ten undergraduate students who had received one week of training in meditation.

Researchers found that while engaging in meditation on the quality of compassion, the monks' brains showed substantial increased activity in the left prefrontal cortex (the seat of positive emotions such as happiness and compassion) and far less activity in the right prefrontal (site of negative emotions and anxiety). In the brains of the novice meditators there was only a slight increase in these "happiness, compassion" areas during meditation. Strikingly, even while not meditating, the monks' brains were different than those of the nonmeditators. These differences suggest that the resting state of the brain may be altered by long-term meditative practice. Richard Davidson, the lead researcher, says, "the fact that monks with the most hours of meditation showed the greatest brain changes—the more practice, the greater the increase in [the brain activity in the left prefrontal part of the brain]—gives us confidence that the changes are actually produced by mental training." (Antoine Lutz, Lawrence L. Greischar, Nancy B. Rawlings, Matthieu Ricard, and Richard J. Davidson, "Long-Term Meditators Self-Induce High-Amplitude Gamma Synchrony During Mental Practice," *PNAS* Proceedings of the National Academy of Sciences. 101, no. 46, November 16, 2004: 16,369–16,373.)

twenty-one years of repeatedly telling yourself that you can never lose weight and twenty-one years of actions that keep you overweight. That neuropathway is going to look like the Grand Canyon!

So, a single session of "I'm slim and healthy" will not do the trick. To instill a new belief that the brain will throw its power behind, your new belief needs to be repeated and experienced numerous times. Regular ten-minute rewiring sessions are particularly potent because we are bringing all of our focus and awareness to them.

It's also important to cleanse your old limiting belief and to repeat your new belief during the course of a normal day. Initially, you may need some reminders, a post-it note on your desk, or a message on your refrigerator. When you find yourself expressing your old belief, it's important to pause, breathe, release it, and remember the feeling of your new belief in your body. State your new belief to yourself, experiencing as much feeling with it as possible. Using your trigger (the special reminder word, phrase, or physical action) can kick-start the experience. For instance, when our dieter catches herself complaining about her chunky thighs, she can stop and breathe deeply to release the angst of that complaint. Then she can stand tall and feel her "slim, healthy" posture as she reminds herself that she is "the perfect weight and in perfect health."

It's important, too, to prepare yourself when you know you are headed into a situation that activates your old conditioned belief. For instance, a family holiday dinner may be a particularly dangerous meal for someone trying to lose weight. Before entering the situation, spend a little time rehearsing your brain: Imagine being at the table feeling confident and proud of the food you are eating. Practice the perfect response to "Just have a little more" or "What? You don't like my cooking?" Picture other aspects of the gathering that will be enjoyable: the conversation and laughter, festive music, and decorations. Whether you are totally successful in maintaining your diet at that particular holiday dinner or not, your brain will have experienced some good rehearsal time to strengthen your new belief.

Let's Get Physical

A conditioned belief also becomes powerful because it is entrenched into our physiology so firmly that any action or thought that does not match up feels weird and wrong. To our unsuccessful dieter, passing up dessert might feel awkward, wasteful, or rude. Regular exercise might feel painful, boring, or even dangerous. Shopping outside the Plus Size Department might feel like a betrayal of her plus-sized friends and family! Her body is signaling her that she is moving outside her comfort zone, the invisible cage that her brain and body know is safe and secure. It's her physiology telling her that something is not aligned with her conditioned belief, that she is an overweight person and should remain so.

A new belief must be as visceral as the old one. This is where a vibrant imagination can be helpful. As you rehearse your new belief in your mind, it's extremely important to engage your body. As our dieter imagines being slim and trim, she needs to feel her flat, taut tummy, her slim, well-shaped arms, her trim and toned calves. She needs to feel how gracefully she would walk, how comfortably she would sit, how naturally erect her posture would be as she stands. She needs to experience how a light meal makes her body feel energetic and satisfies her hunger. Her entire body must become engaged in her slim and trim image to effectively carve her new neuropathway.

Emotionally Attached

Another way our unconscious limited beliefs gained power was by their emotional component, those strong feelings attached to a story. The belief that "I'm just a heavy person" is not only a random, fleeting statement. It has strong emotions holding it in place, such as sadness: "I'll never have the healthy body that other people have. I'll never look as beautiful as those models." Anger: "It's not fair that I was born big. Those little skinny people have no idea how it feels. Our culture is just too weight-conscious." Fear: "What if losing weight causes health problems or leaves me with no energy?" "Will my spouse stop loving me if I lose weight?" Hopelessness: "I guess I'll always be this way. No use in trying."

Your new belief will become as powerful as the old one only if you infuse it with the same level of feeling and emotion. These new feelings must be positive and emphatic. Think of infusing your new images with emotions followed by exclamation points! "I'm excited that I am getting healthier

> The brain has an absolutely fabulous system for getting reward signals. Reward is incredibly powerful and drives a lot of the learning we do.
>
> —*Ann M. Graybiel*

every day! I'm thrilled to see that my body is responding to good food and exercise! I love the new look and feel of my body as I get closer to my optimal weight! I feel great that my friends and family see a new me! I'm inspired that my new weight means improved health for me!"

Those are the three critical keys. To become as powerful as your old belief, your new conditioned belief—that new message you want in your brain—must have the same qualities: clear, detailed, and often repeated; imbedded in your physiology; and containing strong feeling attached to a story. Now to help you understand how to put this into practice, here are some examples.

Writer's Block

Jeannette, a successful business owner, was frustrated because for years she had been unable to get herself to sit down and write the book about her family's history she longed to write. Despite writing courses, tips from published authors, and her strong desire to tell the family story, she froze up every time she sat down to write.

Acknowledge: To get to her limiting belief, Jeannette completed the sentence "I can't write this book because _____." After several minutes of filling in the blank, Jeannette decided that the deepest, most relevant reason was that she was "not smart enough to write a book."

Identify: In a quiet space, Jeannette allowed herself to experience the emotions and physical sensations that accompanied "I'm not smart enough to write a book." To get to her feelings fully, she recalled an incident in junior high where a teacher had written "Lousy writing" across her essay in red ink. Jeannette became aware of the emotions of humiliation and embarrassment she had experienced. She discovered an underlying feeling of sadness that made her chest feel tight and her stomach churn. She encouraged these sensations by staying with them and describing them to herself.

> The only way of discovering the limits of the possible is to venture a little way past them into the impossible.
>
> —*Arthur C. Clarke*

Cleanse: Focusing on the feelings, Jeannette used her breath and imagination. As she inhaled, she imagined a healing stream of air surrounding her heart and stomach area. As she exhaled, she felt the feelings dissipate and leave her body. She continued until she felt a lessening of her emotions' grip on her body.

Insert a New Truth: Still breathing deeply, Jeannette stated her new belief—"I have all the intelligence, resources, and time I need to write this book. Good writing flows effortlessly from me every day." With her statement, Jeannette imagined herself writing with her favorite pen and beautiful writing paper while seated in her most comfortable chair. She felt the fun of remembering her family's history and putting it on paper. She experienced the satisfaction of reviewing completed chapters. She felt her creative juices flowing as words rushed onto the pages. (Later, as Jeannette felt more secure with this image, she imagined other scenes, such as getting a call from a publisher praising her completed work, reading the final published version to her favorite aunt, and speaking to audiences about her family's history and her book.) The trigger Jeannette created was "Emily Dickinson." Whenever she said "Emily Dickinson" she felt her confidence rise and her creativity come alive.

Competitive Drive

Bill was a golf professional at a local course who had always dreamed of playing on the tour. But though his skills were extraordinary, he tended to freeze up during competition, finding himself beaten time and again by those with less talent.

> It is the mark of an educated mind to be able to entertain a thought without accepting it.
>
> —*Aristotle*

Acknowledge: Bill's limiting belief was clear from the start, "I just don't have the competitive fire to do well in tournaments." The trick was to help Bill see that this statement was false! With years of "proof" under his belt and the agreement of his family and peers, this "belief'" seemed to be an undeniable fact. Bill was not initially able to accept that this belief was false, but he softened it by realizing that others who didn't seem to have competitive fire were still able to succeed in competition. In other words, we couldn't convince Bill that he had competitive fire, but we could get him to think that it might not be necessary in order for him to succeed.

Identify: To unearth the feelings beneath Bill's belief, he imagined being in a competitive situation and stating the belief out loud: "I just don't have enough competitive fire." He instantly felt hopeless and discouraged. His limbs felt somewhat lifeless and his thoughts began to race, second guessing his club selection, his read of the greens and distance. "I feel like I've sped up internally but my movements are sluggish, stuck in a fog."

Cleanse: Staying with the image, Bill breathed into these feelings. A visual person, he saw soft purple air surrounding and calming his emotions and thoughts. He saw vibrant yellow air energizing his limbs and muscles. On his exhale, Bill saw gray toxins being released from his body and head.

Insert a New Truth: Rather than a statement encouraging "competitive fire," Bill chose the following: "I have the perfect temperament to be successful on the course. I am calm, analytical, and intuitive, and my body responds to competitive situations with natural power and grace." Bill began by imagining friendly competitions on the golf course with amateur friends and family. He felt his body as relaxed, yet strong, and felt the joy of playing risky shots that normally he avoided. He experienced how brilliantly he was able to read and execute tricky putts, and the satisfaction of collecting on a two dollar Nassau! (When Bill felt comfortable with this image, he upped the ante to club tournaments, city tournaments, then PGA Qualifying School.)

Bill chose the trigger of "old pro." This made him feel seasoned, savvy, and mature. Whenever Bill felt anxiety during a round, "old pro" would infuse him with a sense of confidence and calm.

Calming the Tasmanian Devil

Steven was a self-employed salesman in an urban area, whose marriage was falling apart. His wife worked as his administrative assistant, invoicing, scheduling appointments, and getting directions from customers that Steven needed to visit. But his wife did not always get these directions right. When this happened, Steven exploded and became verbally abusive.

Acknowledge: Initially, of course, Steven figured his marital issues would disappear if his wife simply got the directions right. It took a while for him to realize that his response to the situation was at least part of the problem. Steven filled out a few sheets of "I get so angry when her directions are wrong because _____." Finally, he realized that his belief was that, if she truly loved him, she would make sure the directions were correct—an insight that totally surprised his wife! So Steven's statement of belief was, "When my wife is careless with directions, it means she doesn't love me."

Identify: Once Steven uncovered this belief, the feelings came fairly easily. "My wife doesn't love me" brought forth an extreme sadness and a sense of abandonment. Steven felt vulnerable and helpless. He experienced aching in his chest and tight throat and jaw.

Cleanse: Though it was not easy for him, Steven stayed with the feelings and allowed his deep breathing to cleanse them. Without images, he focused on the breath itself and the relaxation and relief he felt in his body.

Insert a New Truth: Steven's statement became, "My wife's love for me is steady. No matter what happens or what mistakes are made, I know she is there for me." Initially, Steven used his breathing, this statement, and

> It is the mark of an educated mind to be able to entertain a thought without accepting it.
>
> —*Aristotle*

images of loving, relaxed scenes with his wife. He remembered nice dinners she had served him, special presents she had made for him, quiet walks together. When these images came easily to him, Steven threw in a few scenes of discord, continuing his breathing and imagining himself still feeling loved and supported.

The trigger that resonated most with Steven was "I am safe." Whenever he felt his anger rise with his wife or in other situations, "I am safe" instantly brought a sense of peace and control. By using his trigger, Steven was able to step back from the situation and assess it more consciously. In cases where his anger was warranted, he was able to express it more clearly and calmly.

> Man is so made that when anything fires his soul, impossibilities vanish.
>
> —*Jean de la Fontaine*

Note: In Steven's case, there were some deep-rooted childhood traumas that had initiated his conditioned belief of being unloved and abandoned. To cleanse his system of those painful memories, Steven used the same four steps: acknowledging the beliefs that came from those memories, identifying and experiencing the feelings underlying them, cleansing these feelings using breath, and inserting a new positive belief.

Bridging the Chasm

In the first chapter, we talked about the chasm, that huge, seemingly impossible distance between you and your goal that your old conditioned beliefs create. As you begin to rewire your brain, this chasm will appear, often accompanied by feelings of fear or discouragement. Here are ten tips to help bridge the chasm and help you on your way:

- *Why is this goal important to you?* In Chapter 1, I asked you to investigate the real motive underlying your desire. It doesn't matter what others think about it, this motive should be compelling for you. Go back to the exercise in Chapter 1. Write your goal and the motivation for it on an index card and keep it in front of you.

> I have had dreams and I have had nightmares, but I have conquered my nightmares because of my dreams.
>
> —*Dr. Jonas Salk*

- *Just do it!* How often do we tell ourselves that we'll take steps toward our goals and dreams "when we have extra time?" When do we ever have extra time? We only have time for those things that we've determined are priorities. If you really want to experience the benefits of rewiring your brain, your practice sessions will need to become one of those priorities. Put them on your To Do list and schedule them in your day planner. In truth, any of us can find an extra ten to twenty minutes in our day. But if necessary, wouldn't it be worth it to wake up ten to twenty minutes earlier to condition your brain to work for you, not against you?

- *Make practice times pleasurable.* Doing the four-step practice should never feel like a grind! When you work with the steps, do it in an environment that is pleasant to you—maybe with music

> Much good work is lost for the lack of a little more.
>
> —*Edward Harriman*

playing in the background or lighted candles. Make sure that the images you create of your new belief are fun and invigorating. Focus with the same fascinated intensity you feel while watching your favorite sports event or theatrical event.

We don't flake out on our physical exercise routines because they are such hard work. We resist them because they aren't fun! Hiking in the mountains or playing a round of golf can be strenuous as well. But if we have fun with those activities, we're eager to do them. Make your practice times fun enough so that you feel that same sense of eagerness to do them.

1.   *Be persistent and consistent!* Your conditioned pattern didn't just start last week. It's probably been with you for years. Odds are good that it won't be replaced with a new pattern on your very first attempt—or your fifth. When you first use the four-step practice, you may not experience any great changes in your life. In fact, you may become even more painfully aware of the old negative conditioning you want to replace!

> A man will be imprisoned in a room with a door that's unlocked and opens inwards; as long as it does not occur to him to pull rather than push.
>
> —*Ludwig Wittgenstein*

Make a deal with yourself to do the practice for thirty days straight, no matter what. And during those thirty days, be as consistent as you can be about the time of day and amount of time you dedicate to your practice. At the end of thirty days, assess your progress and decide whether to continue or not. It's that simple.

2.   *Focus on just one issue at a time.* Many of us have multiple improvements we would like to make to our lives or goals we would like to pursue. But tackling too many conditioned beliefs at once can scatter your focus and frustrate your brain! Choose one issue. If you have experience with this type of self-work, you may want to start with a desire that seems most urgent or a conditioned belief that has become the biggest obstacle in your life. If you are new to this type of work, you may want to begin with a smaller desire, one that seems more within your reach than others, or with a conditioned belief that is irritating but not extremely upsetting. By starting small, you can become a student of the process and become more proficient before tackling larger issues. Even-

> A goal without a plan is just a wish.
>
> —*Antoine de Saint-Exupery*

tually it will be like a domino effect—your brain will begin supporting all new empowering beliefs, actions, desires.

Work with that one issue for a period of time until you feel that it has shifted. The definition of

EXERCISE: Sixty Seconds to Momentum

The most difficult thing about any endeavor—exercising, a project at work or home, studying—is starting, getting through our inertia to get moving! But we can all get ourselves to do something for just sixty seconds. I may not be eager to go running. But when I tell myself that I will just spend sixty seconds getting prepared to run, by the time I've tied my shoes I'm ready to go! When you feel that sluggish resistance to practicing your four steps, tell yourself that you will just spend sixty seconds preparing for it: going to your quiet place, sitting down, pulling out your notes on the belief you are processing. Odds are good that you'll feel ready to get down to business quickly!

shift is "moving something to a different position or exchanging one thing for another within the same class." An old conditioned belief has shifted when it feels less real and compelling to you. A new belief has shifted when, despite circumstances, you can easily slip into the experience of it.

Take the example of feeling betrayed. You may initially feel the emotion of deep resentment accompanied by hurt. You may experience its presence in your body as tension in the neck, pinched throat, ache in the chest. As you breathe deeply with these feelings, they will change: resentment and hurt may turn to sadness and finally a sense of calm. Your body will relax. As you begin your new empowering image of being safe and secure, it may be pleasant but faint.

The next time you work with this issue, your negative feelings may be less intense, you may move more quickly to a relaxed state of peace. Your new image may be more alive and have more depth of pleasant feelings. Over several sessions, you

> Our greatest glory is not in never falling, but in rising up every time we fall.
>
> —*Confucius*

> Whatever course you decide upon, there is always someone to tell you that you are wrong. There are always difficulties arising which tempt you to believe that your critics are right. To map out a course of action and follow it to an end requires courage.
>
> —*Ralph Waldo Emerson*

may notice that it is easy to transition from your old story to your new belief and that your new image is more vibrant and visceral than the old. That's the shift we're seeking.

3. *Incorporate your practice into daily life.* If you spend ten minutes a day with a new positive belief and the other twenty-three hours and fifty minutes mired in your old limiting belief, which will become stronger? As you unearth the limiting stories and beliefs that hold you back, notice when they pop up during your day. Stop, breathe, and use your trigger to get at least a taste of the experience of your new belief. Rehearse your brain prior to entering situations that normally call up your old reactions. Use your breathing to unplug yourself if you slip into an old conditioned pattern that does not serve you.

4. *Use the buddy system.* In Chapter 1, I talked about engaging cheerleaders to help you along the way. It's even more effective to find a buddy who is also committed to rewiring their conditioned beliefs. Set up regular check-in sessions where you can talk about your experience as you practice and acknowledge one another's progress.

   Avoiding negative buddies is as important as surrounding ourselves with positive ones. Our well-meaning friends and family might have bought into the conditioned beliefs we are trying to rewire. They want to protect us, or themselves, by encouraging us to stay in our conditioned cages: "Play it safe." "Don't bite off more than you can chew." "Don't get your hopes up." Their opinions and fears will only feed into your own doubts and limiting beliefs. So as you begin this journey, be especially careful about your interactions with negative buddies.

> Pay no attention to what the critics say. There has never been a statue erected to a critic.
>
> —*Jean Sibelius*

5. *Track your progress.* You bought this book and embarked on this journey because you wanted to achieve certain results. In self-growth, sometimes it's hard to quantify our progress. We may be expanding internally long before we see measurable external results. I recommend keeping a journal to track how far you've come from where you started.

6. *Celebrate!* Celebrate yourself for even embarking on this journey. Give yourself kudos for sticking to it, or, if you fall off the wagon, give yourself kudos for getting back on track. Celebrate your progress. Celebrate your willingness. Give

> Don't judge each day by the harvest you reap, but by the seeds you plant.
>
> —*Robert Louis Stevenson*

yourself a treat for making it through an entire week of practice. Congratulate yourself for catching yourself right before you fall into an old conditioned pattern. Pat yourself on the back for doing your deep breathing before you go to sleep.

Becoming your own conditioner is like becoming your own coach. The greatest coaches are inspiring and acknowledge our attempts and progress. No one performs well for a coach who only points out failings and faults. Encourage yourself the way you would encourage your favorite child.

7. *Let yourself dream!* We touched on this briefly in Chapter 6. The goals and desires you choose for yourself must be yours alone—not those chosen for you by your parents or your peers or your

> Life is a great big canvas, and you should throw all the paint on it you can.
>
> —*Danny Kaye*

EXERCISE: **Progress Report**

A good way to track your progress is to answer the same group of questions at different phases and compare your answers. Though internal progress is not really quantifiable, it helps to rank your experience on a scale of one to ten. Use the following questions as a guideline. You may want to develop others on your own.

On a scale of one to ten:

1. How strong does my old belief feel?
2. How much does it impact my life?
3. How easy is it to recognize my old patterns when they come up in daily situations?
4. How able am I to pause, breathe, and release my old conditioned reactions?
5. How real does my new belief feel?
6. How experiential are my practice times?
7. How regularly do I incorporate this new experience into my daily life?

spouse. Your brain can be (and has been) conditioned with any belief or story. Your brain doesn't care what is planted in it and will work equally hard to support beliefs that are positive, negative, your own, or someone else's. By taking conscious charge of your own conditioning, you have the opportunity to harness the power of your brain to create a new reality for yourself. Make sure it's one that you choose.

I also encourage you to dream big. We don't really know what is possible for us. The limitations that our conditioning has set for us are not real. I don't know if you can start a singing career at fifty-seven and make a go of it. I don't know if you can start a part-time, home-based business and become a millionaire within two years. I don't know if you can heal the relationship with

Hell is living someone else's life.

—*Joseph Campbell*

your spouse and children and live a fabulous life together. I don't know if you can lose those pounds, learn that language, win that match, write that novel.

But I do know this: limiting conditioned beliefs within your brain have created an invisible cage for you. Based on these beliefs, your brain has worked very hard to keep you in this cage and assert its reality. And I know that once you dissolve that cage and harness the power of your brain in the direction you choose, it will work equally hard to create your new reality.

And I know that you now have the tools to do it.

> If no one ever took risks, Michelangelo would have painted the Sistine floor.
>
> —*Neil Simon*

> The very least you can do in your life is to figure out what you hope for. And the most you can do is live inside that hope. Not admire it from a distance but live right in it, under its roof.
>
> —*Barbara Kingsolver*

Beyond Conditioning

As a psychologist, sometimes I get caught up in the mechanics of conditioning and how we can use it consciously to improve our lives. But I don't believe that the ultimate goal of expanding our human potential is just to exchange one cage for a bigger, brighter one. The ultimate goal, our ultimate potential, is to be cageless. It is only when we are cageless that we can experience our full, intrinsic power.

Enlightenment, pure consciousness, Nirvana, living in the now, pure presence, egolessness: These concepts of cagelessness seem too vague and too grand to have practical meaning for many of us. But there is a contemporary concept that more of us can relate to: being in the zone.

We usually hear about "being in the zone" or "being in the flow" in reference to athletic or artistic endeavors. It's the place from which peak performance is born. In this place, temporal concerns (time, food, ego-self) are suspended. Everything in your experience, how you perceive your surroundings, your sensations, thoughts, and actions all seem to slow down. In the zone, you experience hyper mental clarity and focus. Your entire system is in synch, creating decisive purposeful action, flowing and appropriate movement.

Psychologist and author of *Finding Flow,* Mihaly Csikszentmihalyi is one of the world's leading researchers on those cageless moments of being in the flow. He describes the experience of flow as "being completely involved in an activity for its own sake. The ego falls away. Time flies. Every action, movement, and thought follows inevitably from the previous one, like playing jazz. Your whole being is involved, and you're using your skills to the utmost." Typical sources for the experience of flow are creative activities, play, music, sports, games, and religious rituals.

Csikszentmihalyi interviewed more than 10,000 people from around the world, asking them to describe how they feel when they are thoroughly involved in something that is enjoyable and meaningful to them. A composer described writing his music as "You are in an ecstatic state to such a point that you feel as though you almost don't exist. . . . My hand seems devoid of myself, and I have nothing to do with what is happening. I just sit there watching in a state of awe and wonderment. And the music just flows out by itself." A well-know lyricist and former poet laureate of the United States described a similar feeling while writing: "You lose your sense of time, you're completely enraptured, you are completely caught up in what you're doing, and you are sort of swayed by the possibilities you see in this work. If that becomes too powerful, then you get up, because the excitement is too great. . . . The idea is to be so, so saturated with it that there's no future or past, it's just an extended present in which you are . . . making meaning. And dismantling meaning, and remaking it."

Others who have researched this phenomenon have focused on athletes. James Loehr asked over three hundred athletes to describe their finest hour in sports. From this data, Loehr identified twelve ideal qualities of internal experience for optimal athletic performance: physically relaxed, mentally calm, low anxiety, energized, optimistic, enjoyment, effortless, automatic, alert, mentally focused, self-confident, and in control. Charles Garfield and

Hal Zina Bennett conducted a similar study of elite athletes and identified eight mental and physical conditions that they labeled "peak performance feelings": mentally alert, physically relaxed, confident and optimistic with a generally positive outlook, focused on the present, highly energized, extraordinary awareness, in control, and in the "cocoon" without fear or anxiety.

Being in the flow is not only reported by composers, writers, and athletes, but also by students who love studying, parents who love spending time with their children, workers who love their work, gardeners who love gardening. The zone is often thought of as a state that mysteriously happens to someone out of the blue. But within our daily lives, we have all experienced this cagelessness, those certain moments when we are fully present and alive. Moments when our conditioning, positive or negative, takes a backseat to a force within us that is purer, more expansive, and wise. Sometimes the experience is dramatic. You stepped into the flow during a crisis that required immediate action. Suddenly, you find that you are emotionally calm, mentally focused, able to act swiftly and appropriately to handle whatever is necessary in the situation. It is only after the crisis is resolved that you feel fear, panic, and upset.

Intuitively, we can feel how these cageless moments enhance our health, mental clarity, creative abilities, and our emotional well-being. You may have experienced this state while making love, when time seemed to slow down and you felt your entire being completely immersed in the wonderful sensations and heart-expanding emotion of those moments. You may have experienced this state while running a marathon or after giving birth. The zone is *not* reserved for peak performers.

But what most peak performers know is that they can access the zone, this cageless experience, *at will*. In truth, perhaps this is one of the main differences between peak performers and others: peak perform-

> People are happy not because of what they do, but because of how they do it.
>
> —*Mihaly Csikszentmihalyi*

> A moment is a concentrated eternity.
>
> —*Ralph Waldo Emerson*

ers enter the zone and work with the flow intentionally and more frequently than others of equal talent and ability.

Even without the training of a top athlete or insight of a creative genius, we all have easy access to such moments. We naturally enter a powerful flow, a type of zone, whenever we give ourselves over to the powers of beauty, joy, play, love, or appreciation.

Carried Away by Beauty

We've all felt the cageless experience of beauty: listening to a wonderful piece of music, walking through a magnificent forest or lovely meadow, viewing a timeless painting, or watching an exquisite dance troupe. When we pause in the busy-ness of our days and take a moment to observe, we can also find beauty in the smallest moments: the gentle snore of a baby, the light as it scatters through a dusty window, the scent of bread in the oven, the grace of a cat curling up to sleep.

> Beauty is but the sensible image of the Infinite. Like truth and justice it lives within us; like virtue and the moral law it is a companion of the soul.
>
> —*George Bancroft*

Beauty, when we stop to find it, is everywhere. During the moments when we pause and allow beauty to seep into our being, we are lifted out of ourselves and our conditioned responses. We feel expansive and vibrant, connected to something greater than our individual selves. In these moments, we feel the pulsing of possibility lighting up all of our circuits!

Joy to the World!

Joy is defined as "feelings of great happiness or pleasure, especially of an elevated or spiritual kind." For me it is an unfettered, almost giddy feeling that takes over my entire body. It is the uncontrollable laughter at a movie

---

EXERCISE: **Beauty Rest**

Stepping into moments of beauty is powerful for recharging the body, brain, and spirit. Plan regular beauty breaks within your normal routine: a few minutes first thing in the morning to listen to wonderful music, a quick walk outdoors in the afternoon, a few pages of poetry before you lay your head on the pillow. Use beauty as the foreground, not the background. In other words, don't spend your moments of walking in nature untangling a knotty problem from work! To reap the most benefit during these beauty breaks, really bring your focus to the beauty itself.

---

or a friend's joke. It is the sheer delight of seeing a long-lost friend or a new puppy. It is the impulsive fun of dancing in the kitchen or eating my favorite ice cream. Like beauty, joy is all around us and available in any moment when we turn our attention to it.

> Some cause happiness wherever they go; others whenever they go.
>
> —*Oscar Wilde*

Is it really possible to feel joy during trying times and in difficult circumstances? Yes. Joy is always an option and a good choice to make if you wish to live a full and healthy life. This is not to infer that you will feel joyful *about* your difficult circumstances. When a loved one has died, you will feel deeply sad, not happy about it. But your grieving does not prevent you from feeling joy about other areas of your life: the loved ones still with you, your wonderful memories of the person you have lost, your own health and well-being.

Doesn't our common sense tell us that happiness and joy are good for us? When we've spent a girls' night out or a guys' night out laughing with our buddies, we feel great, physically alive, optimistic, expansive. When we watch the *Three Stooges* or goofy cartoons,

> People often say that "beauty is in the eye of the beholder," and I say that the most liberating thing about beauty is realizing that you are the beholder. This empowers us to find beauty in places where others have not dared to look, including inside ourselves.
>
> —*Salma Hayek*

> It is only possible to live happily ever after on a day-to-day basis.
>
> —*Margaret Bonnano*

we feel our tension release and our mood rise. The glow of these moments of joy stays with us, making our sleep more peaceful and our daily activities more enjoyable.

Playing Around

When we play, we free ourselves from the concerns of daily life and throw ourselves into a pleasurable activity, like a sport or a hobby. Just like qualities of being in the zone, we feel immersed in the activity, our focus is total yet relaxed, time has no meaning. Even if the activity is strenuous or requires concentration, because it is "play" to us, it leaves us feeling invigorated and alive. Compare an evening of doing your favorite hobby (maybe singing, playing chess, or building model trains) or playing your favorite sport to a normal day at work. Which leaves you feeling more vibrant and excited about life?

> Life can be hard and fate can seem cruel, but happiness is always an option.
>
> —*Dean Koontz*

Within the work ethic of modern Western culture, the experiences of beauty, joy, or play seem to be nonproductive, wasteful activities that we should allow ourselves only after all the work is done (which it rarely is!). Especially when times are tough, we view such things as frivolous and distracting. Yet research has found that allowing ourselves to be in these cageless zone moments has many practical applications and benefits. The work ethic that keeps our noses to the grindstone is actually causing us to be less effective at taking care of business and finding intelligent solutions!

> The aging process has you firmly in its grasp if you never get the urge to throw a snowball.
>
> —*Doug Larson*

EXERCISE: **Tap the Joy**

In truth, joy resides within us, not outside of us. But it helps to find outside triggers to remind us to experience joy on a daily basis. Here are some questions to help you discover your triggers.

What in your everyday life gives you joy? (Or what, if you paused and took the time to really acknowledge it, in your everyday life *could* give you joy?)

What were joyful activities from your past or your childhood? Could you re-introduce them to your life?

Who is fun in your life? How could you arrange to spend more time with them?

Attitude of Gratitude

Appreciation is defined as "a f eeling of gratefulness about something" and "a full understanding of the meaning and importance of something." Many spiritual traditions emphasize the importance of "a grateful heart," not merely as a virtue but as a path to connect with the Divine. Experienced fully, moments of appreciation open us to the flow and all of the qualities of cageless moments.

Think of someone you love, not all of the nit-picky complaints you have about that person, but focus on his or her wonderful qualities, the gifts he

EXERCISE: **Appreciation by the Alphabet**

Can't think of what you appreciate? Play the alphabet game: for each letter of the alphabet, write down someone or something, no matter how small, that you appreciate. Do not let yourself stop until you've completed the entire list. Try this exercise every day for seven days, never using the same person or item. You'll be amazed at how many people and things you appreciate and how good you feel as you focus on them. Good luck with the letter Z!

> I who am blind can give one hint to those who see: use your eyes as if tomorrow you would be stricken blind. And the same method can be applied to the other senses. Hear the music of voices, the song of a bird, the mighty strains of an orchestra as if you would be stricken deaf tomorrow. Touch each object as if tomorrow your tactile sense would fail. Smell the perfume of flowers, taste with relish each morsel as if tomorrow you could never smell and taste again. Make the most of every sense, glory in all the facets of pleasure and beauty which the world reveals to you through the several means of contact which nature provides.
>
> —*Helen Keller*

or she brings to the world and how he or she has enhanced your life. As you allow appreciation to well up inside you, how do you feel physically, mentally, emotionally?

Take a moment to think about your life circumstances, not all that is lacking or missing, but all that is good and present in your life. Let your sense of appreciation expand to your past and its wonderful moments and significant lessons. As you step fully into this experience, you open the door to the calm, optimism, confidence, and well-being of the flow.

What's the Point?

My purpose for this book and all of my work is to help people break free of the cage of their negative conditioning. It is this cage that prevents us from living the rich lives we all desire. It is this cage that keeps us in lives that are smaller than our dreams, lives that seem to lack meaning.

Many of us have had glimpses of our potential. But within this cage, we felt controlled and confined. We found ourselves fighting to be free of barriers that we couldn't see and didn't understand, our unconscious conditioning.

My mission is to bring the barriers of your limiting conditioning to your awareness so you can consciously choose whether to maintain that conditioning or rewire it. It is your choice to either allow your brain's power to work against your dreams and goals based on prior limiting beliefs, or to create new empowering conditioned beliefs to redirect your brain's power so you can be, do, and have what you desire. It is also your choice to either remain within a caged realm of thoughts, emotions, and actions or to expand your experience with cageless moments of flow.

I support you in all of your choices.

Adrianne Ahern

ABOUT THE AUTHOR

ADRIANNE AHERN has earned two masters degrees, and a PhD in clinical psychology. Dr Ahern lectures and leads workshops throughout the country on her Snap Out of It Now! Method, described in this book and her previous one, *Snap Out of It Now!* Her breakthrough methodology for re-wiring the brain was developed over the last fifteen years through her work with hundreds of clients both in her private practice and in her consulting role at prestigious Scripps Hospital in La Jolla, California.

Drawing on advanced research on human potential and the recent discoveries about how the brain functions, Dr. Ahern developed effective tools that integrate the disciplines of psychology, psychophysiology, neurofeedback and personal achievement analysis. A frequent guest on both television and radio, Dr. A presents this complex material with wit and clarity, helping her audiences and readers to bridge the gaps between heart, mind and body to overcome barriers and unleash potential.

Sentient Publications, LLC publishes books on cultural creativity, experimental education, transformative spirituality, holistic health, new science, ecology, and other topics, approached from an integral viewpoint. Our authors are intensely interested in exploring the nature of life from fresh perspectives, addressing life's great questions, and fostering the full expression of human potential. Sentient Publications' books arise from the spirit of inquiry and the richness of the inherent dialogue between writer and reader.

Our Culture Tools series is designed to give social catalyzers and cultural entrepreneurs the essential information, technology, and inspiration to forge a sustainable, creative, and compassionate world.

We are very interested in hearing from our readers. To direct suggestions or comments to us, or to be added to our mailing list, please contact:

SENTIENT PUBLICATIONS, LLC
1113 Spruce Street
Boulder, CO 80302
303-443-2188
contact@sentientpublications.com
www.sentientpublications.com